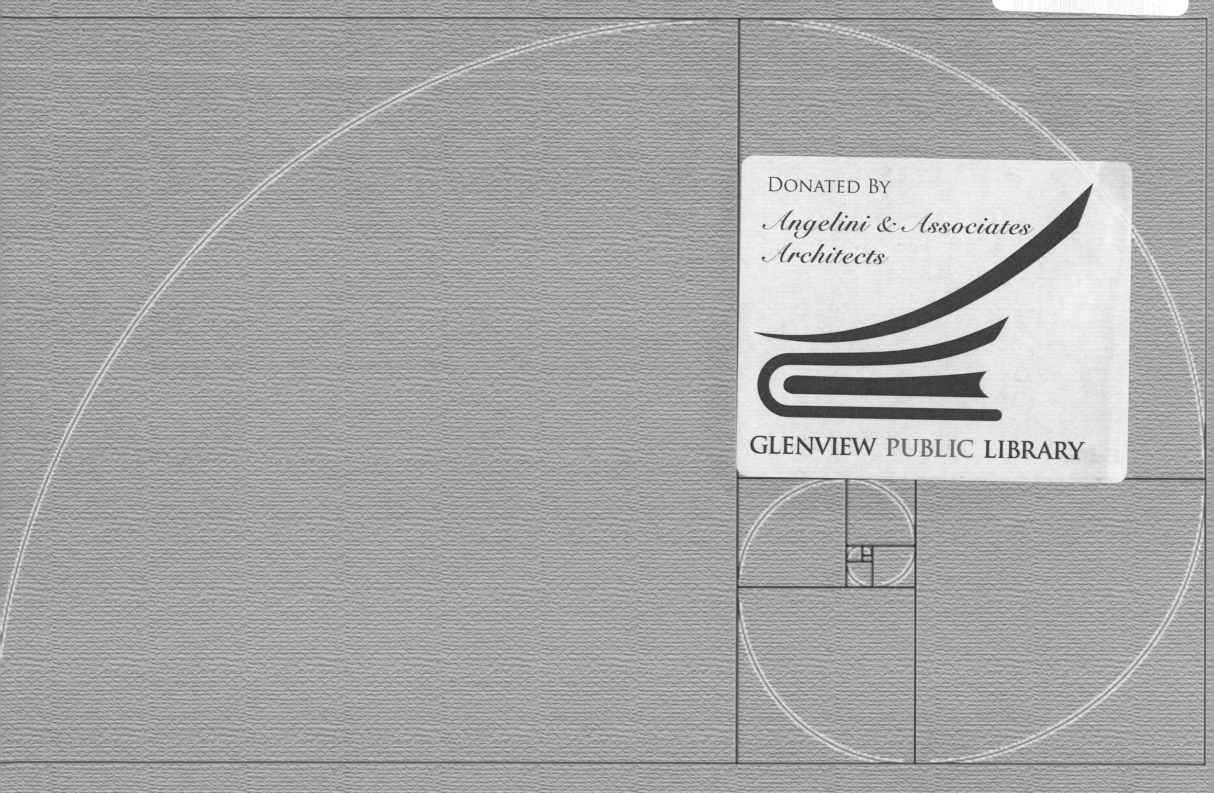

DREAM HOMES

MICHIGAN

AN EXCLUSIVE SHOWCASE OF MICHIGAN'S FINEST ARCHITECTS, DESIGNERS AND BUILDERS

Published by

PANACHE

PANACHE PARTNERS, LLC

1424 Gables Court
Plano, Texas 75075
469.246.6060
f: 469.246.6062
www.panache.com

Publishers: Brian G. Carabet and John A. Shand

Printed in Malaysia

Distributed by IPG
800.748.5439

PUBLISHER'S DATA

Dream Homes Michigan

Library of Congress Control Number: 2008920705

ISBN -13:   978-1-933415-09-3
ISBN -10:   1-933415-09-6

First Printing 2008

10 9 8 7 6 5 4 3 2 1

Previous Page: Tobias Construction, Inc., page 173
Photograph by Josh Tobias

Right: Thomas Sebold & Associates, Inc., page 161
Alexander V. Bogaerts + Associates, page 61
Photograph by Michael Buck Studio

DREAM HOMES
MICHIGAN

AN EXCLUSIVE SHOWCASE OF MICHIGAN'S FINEST ARCHITECTS, DESIGNERS AND BUILDERS

Young & Young Architects, Inc., page 207

INTRODUCTION

Clifford N. Wright Associates Architects, page 51

Home to some of the most innovative, gifted and dedicated designers and builders in the nation, the state of Michigan has long been treasured for its scenery, seasons and traditions of craftsmanship, which have lured creative minds at the top of their professions to the Great Lakes State.

Bounded by four of the five Great Lakes, Michigan boasts the longest freshwater shoreline in the world and is adorned with a diversity of inland lakes, hills and majestic dunes. This unique canvas has afforded an ideal backdrop for skilled professionals to place their enduring works of art—the dream home.

Buoyed by unflagging zest, *Dream Homes Michigan* is a remarkable compilation featuring the work and philosophies of highly regarded architects, designers and builders. The accomplished professionals featured on the pages that follow were chosen for their talent, artistry and command of craft. From classical and traditional to aggressively contemporary, their captivating homes display thoughtful, sophisticated designs that epitomize the homeowner's lifestyles and stylistic proclivities. Each home represents a melding of the creator's vast knowledge and experience, attention to detail and aesthetic sensibility coupled with hard work and a bona fide passion for superiorly designed and crafted architecture.

DesRosiers Architects, page 75

From small additions to elaborate renovations, restorations and, of course, new construction projects, the featured homes grace the Lower Peninsula from Grand Rapids, Ann Arbor and the affluent suburbs of Oakland Country, to the shimmering shores of Harbor Springs, Charlevoix and Grand Traverse Bay and everywhere in between.

The beautiful homes on the pages that follow display the talents of Michigan's finest architects, designers and builders, yet the men and women of *Dream Homes Michigan* measure their success through the happiness of their clients.

Angelini & Associates Architects, page 47

Enjoy!

Brian Carabet and John Shand
Publishers

FOREWORD

Don Paul Young

We who create architecture in the state of Michigan are a very privileged and dedicated group of professionals. The patron, architects and construction team—scores of artisans and craftsmen—engage in the process of building a dream, which is often an experience lasting many months or years. All of this effort is to create architecture of eternal values that will enhance the lives of our clients and be respectful of planet Earth.

In Michigan, it is understood that we must properly overcome the construction difficulties of building in sun, wind, rain, ice and snow—and temperatures that vary from -10 degrees to 110 degrees Fahrenheit. Of course, we readily assume responsibility, knowing that the completed "dream home" and its sensitive, natural marriage to the site will allow our clients to intimately enjoy the ever-changing beauty of our seasons and life in Michigan.

The breathtaking beauty and diverse characteristics of building sites in Michigan are remarkable. The landscape is varied and includes remote forests; our Great Lakes; large and small inland lakes and rivers; prairies; rolling country; and the charm of our historic urban and suburban environments, all of which provide wonderful opportunities. The uniqueness and location of the building site will ultimately influence the client in his or her selection of an architect whose philosophy is proper for these circumstances.

The residences showcased in *Dream Homes Michigan* offer a great many stylistic influences: classical, historical, traditional, modern, contemporary and a few unnamed styles. Any one of these styles may create a completely new lifestyle experience for the client. An architect's preliminary vision of the "dream home" is not just the home itself, but the development of the entire site from lot line to lot line. Therefore the preliminary concept not only addresses the

DesRosiers Architects, page 75, *Photograph by Glen Rauth*

Visbeen Associates, Inc., page 187

DesRosiers Architects, page 75, *Photograph by Laszlo Regos*

interior spaces but how those interior elements relate to exterior requirements such as terraces, swimming pools, driveways, arrival courts, water features and so on. He must then determine how all of these elements may celebrate or protect us from our environment, whether it is natural or built. His vision then weaves the required spaces, furnishings, artifacts and the building site into one harmonious concept—with the creation of interior spaces that become experiential, poetic and uplifting being the basis of the entire design. Architecture, to be fully appreciated, requires movement and motion and every design must be planned to be never-ending so that one experiences the continuous melding of all spaces—interior and exterior, the site and distant views as one significant composition.

The beautiful homes on the following pages showcase the immense talents of the architects, designers, builders and a multitude of artisans and craftsmen devoted to excellence and the realization of dreams in this great state.

Don Paul Young, AIA Emeritus

The Cottage Company of Harbor Springs, page 125

Widing Custom Homes, Inc., page 199

BRG Custom Homes, page 55

CONTENTS

MICHIGAN

BRG Custom Homes, page 55

Dominick Tringali Architects, Inc., page 177

Alexander V. Bogaerts + Associates, page 61

"The yearning for the cottage isn't necessarily a solitary quest for a quiet, rustic retreat. Perhaps it is more a harmonic blending of serene beauty, family and close friends; the making of many colorful memories, like a patchwork quilt, that when sewn together warms us as the years march on."

—*Karen Winters*

DesRosiers Architects, page 75, *Photograph by Beth Singer*   CBi Design Professionals, Inc., page 71

"There are wonderful ways of presenting things—and that's what architecture is about, the art of presentation. Every time you turn a corner it's the art of presentation of that space."

—*Don Paul Young*

Thomas Sebold & Associates, Inc., page 161

Architectural Resource, page 103

DesRosiers Architects, page 75, *Photograph by George Dzahristos*

AZD Associates Inc.-Architects, page 37

"Architecture is about creating an environment that is responsive to human values. It's not about systems, materials, structure—in the end, it's about how you respond to the human being."

—*Robert L. Ziegelman*

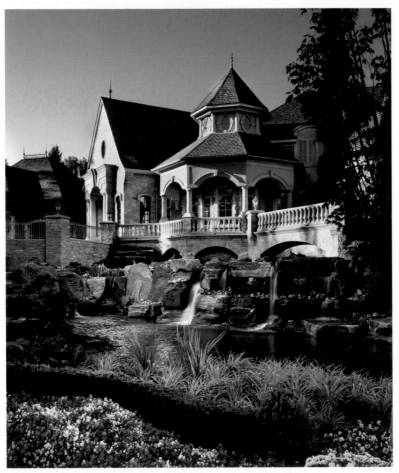

Dominick Tringali Architects, Inc., page 177

Thomas Sebold & Associates, Inc., page 161
Young & Young Architects, Inc., page 207

"When you come home to your residence, whether it's the first day or 10 years later, going up the driveway should be just as exciting for you then as the very first time."

—*Louis DesRosiers*

Visbeen Associates, Inc., page 187

Victor Saroki & Associates Architects PC, page 153

Young & Young Architects, Inc., page 207

Young & Young Architects, Inc., page 207
Thomas Sebold & Associates, Inc., page 161

MICHIGAN

NATHAN ABBOTT
DUSTIN CARPENTER

Falcon Custom Homes, Inc.

Just as the falcon—a symbol of pride, strength and ability—acts deliberately with speed and precision, so too does the talented team of professionals at Falcon Custom Homes, Inc. Started by partners Nathan Abbott and Dustin Carpenter, Falcon Custom Homes, Inc. is an innovative firm bringing original products, ideas and unique floorplans to each exquisite home it builds. Graduates of Michigan State's award-winning construction management program, Nathan and Dustin bring great building knowledge and project management skills to every job the firm undertakes. Falcon Custom Homes, Inc. is eager to tackle new and challenging projects that bring out the best in its staff, and the firm's sophisticated homes are bringing a fresh look to southwestern Michigan—especially the Grand Rapids, Ada and Forest Hill areas—and miles beyond.

ABOVE:
The custom star-shaped, inlaid wood medallion is a focal point of the rich wood floor in this welcoming entryway.
Photograph courtesy of Falcon Custom Homes, Inc.

FACING PAGE:
This majestic waterfront home overlooking Bay Harbor Lake in Petoskey features generous fenestration to take advantage of captivating lake views.
Photograph courtesy of Falcon Custom Homes, Inc.

Homeowners who collaborate with Falcon Custom Homes, Inc. receive the close attention and exacting detail that has resulted in a supremely satisfied customer base that cherishes the effective communication, exceptional quality and ongoing, unmatched service that characterize the homebuilding process. Early in the homebuilding process, clients formulate plans that lead to a unique design, which is constructed on a controlled yet very deliberate schedule. Utilizing only highly skilled subcontractors and craftsmen that meet Falcon Custom Homes, Inc.'s. high standards for consistent quality and results, the firm views its group of subcontractors as a family. Managing the group as an effective unit results in on-time, cost-effective outcomes that delight satisfied homeowners. Moreover, the tried-and-true subcontractor base consistently produces artisan-quality work in an array of locations—the firm builds homes within a three-hour radius of Grand Rapids.

While each home built by Falcon Custom Homes, Inc. is a one-of-a-kind creation, personally tailored to the particular desires and lifestyle requirements of its owner, there are a few hallmarks of the firm's work. Intricate ceiling details, custom cabinetry and extraordinary mouldings

TOP RIGHT:
The natural stone of this massive fireplace is contrasted warmly by the wood mantel, giving visual interest to the centerpiece of this well-appointed living area.
Photograph courtesy of Falcon Custom Homes, Inc.

BOTTOM RIGHT:
The rounded glass door to this upper-level bedroom creates inviting scale, which is further enhanced by the muted browns and generous wood headboard with nightstands within.
Photograph courtesy of Falcon Custom Homes, Inc.

FACING PAGE:
A subtle yet elegant white fireplace separates spaces in this dining area, which includes stately columns, stone floors, rounded arches and a recessed ceiling feature over the chandelier.
Photograph courtesy of Falcon Custom Homes, Inc.

are prevalent features in the firm's creations, and custom requests are encouraged. One home built in Ada, Michigan, included a 400-square-foot dollhouse—inside the larger home—for the homeowners' 7-year-old daughter. The dollhouse had shutters, fine details and was split into two floors that included a kitchen, reading area and dress-up area.

Falcon Custom Homes, Inc. has received its share of awards and recognition—from the public and peers alike. The firm has collected multiple People's Choice Awards each fall since 2004, in addition to recognition by the Sales and Marketing Council of West Michigan. Several elegant homes have been featured on the Home & Building Association of Greater Grand Rapids' Parade of Homes, an annual showcase of phenomenal new residences.

Under the leadership of Nathan and Dustin, Falcon Custom Homes, Inc. has established itself as a first-rate builder dedicated to delivering superior quality homes, carefully crafted by its family of skilled subcontractors that exceed clients' expectations. This talented firm is certain to soar majestically into the future, like a graceful falcon ascending high above the shimmering blue Michigan waters below.

LEFT:
Curvilinear forms abound in this home's two-story front entry—light green plaster and wood flooring create an inconspicuous backdrop for the low-hanging light elements and steeply rising staircase.
Photograph courtesy of Falcon Custom Homes, Inc.

FACING PAGE:
This secluded home delicately blends brick and cedar exterior elements with turrets and pitched roofs to achieve a timeless, classic look.
Photograph courtesy of Falcon Custom Homes, Inc.

Ghassan Abdelnour
Freeman Greer
Al Valentine

GAV & Associates, Inc.

Formed from a pair of independent architectural offices in 1998, GAV & Associates offers vast architectural experience gleaned from years of undertaking a wide array of projects ranging from commercial, educational and industrial, to multi-family and custom residential. But it is the special attention clients receive and dedication to excellence from owners Ghassan Abdelnour, Al Valentine and Freeman Greer, AIA, that set GAV apart.

Combining more than 20 years of architecture experience with their unwavering commitment to customer satisfaction, Ghassan, Al and Freeman take part in the development process from beginning to end, creating a lasting relationship with clients along the way. Moreover, designing an engaging, timeless custom home is not just a priority at GAV & Associates, it is an obligation. For clients, the opportunity to work with Ghassan and his wife Ban, a fellow architect and home design specialist, is more than a business affair; it is the beginning of a lasting friendship. In fact, an ideal Saturday for the couple consists

of visiting former clients in their GAV-designed homes, catching up and ensuring that they're delighted with the results. This gives Ghassan and Ban genuine and lasting fulfillment.

The process begins with extensive consultation between the client and Ghassan and his team, during which, they listen and provide honest advice to precisely ascertain the client's needs. Al and Freeman produce an innovative, structurally sound edifice that elegantly exhibits Ghassan and Ban's design acumen.

While the Farmington Hills-based firm designs custom residences of all shapes, sizes and styles, the most prevalent style is undoubtedly neoclassical, with its enduring elegance and lasting charm. Utilizing grandiose columns, textured, eclectic stones, prodigious arch entrances and detailed windows and gables, they create stately, yet everlasting designs. Moreover, they utilize elevation to showcase the custom residence in a way that commands attention.

TOP LEFT:
The neoclassical entrance is defined by textured, majestic columns, eclectic stones, detailed windows and gables.
Photograph by Hal Kearney

BOTTOM LEFT:
The design of this interior creates synergy between the outside and the sophisticated charm of the interior space.
Photograph by Hal Kearney

FACING PAGE TOP:
Grandiose columns and textured stone contrast the dark stain of the entrance doors to create a stately, timeless design.
Photograph by Ghassan Abdelnour

FACING PAGE BOTTOM:
Rich materials contrast delightfully and procure a warm and refined aura in this custom residence.
Photograph by by Ghassan Abdelnour

Creating synergy between outside and inside, columns and other common elements appear in the front entrance area, welcoming those who enter while bringing that impressive outdoor décor inside the house. That main entrance area, typically two stories, is critical to an exquisite custom design as it, along with the connection to the kitchen and master bedroom, creates vital circulation and harmony.

While GAV & Associates' wide range of projects is essential to weathering economic downturns, it also provides the firm with a wealth of experience essential to tackling diverse projects. However, Ghassan and Ban take the most joy from working diligently with clients to design their ideal custom residence, which is not merely an occupational duty, but a responsibility. "This is the house they're going to live in for the rest of their lives, or very much of it," they relate. "We tell our clients, 'Don't tell us it's good, you have to tell us, I love it.' Every day they walk into that area they need to say, 'Wow, that's so beautiful.'"

Steve Adelaine
Melissa Adelaine
Noah Adelaine

Adelaine Construction, Inc.

Adelaine Construction has been building quality custom homes in northern Michigan for years, thanks largely to President Steve Adelaine's lifelong association with the custom home building industry—his father worked in construction before him—as well as his experience around an array of construction types and exacting attention to detail. He is involved with every project personally and visits each jobsite daily. In recent years, Steve's daughter, Melissa, and son, Noah, have joined the family business, and are helping to grow Adelaine Construction and expand its range of services, always striving to satisfy customers beyond belief.

A family business built on the traditions of old-fashioned craftsmanship with a vision to the future, Adelaine Construction undertakes custom additions/remodels, log, new construction and light commercial projects. When Melissa joined the family business she worked on jobsites as a laborer for five years before moving into the office to handle the sales, marketing and business planning affairs—where her

accounting, business management and marketing degrees allow her to excel. She coordinates each project from concept to completion, and more recently began running the company's computer-aided design program. Maintaining a full-time office presence, she affords clients the luxury of knowing they can always reach a team member.

Recently graduated with a construction management degree with honors, Noah has stepped into his father's position as foreman, controlling quality and production on site. He has brought a wealth of experience and innovative ideas to the family business. Spending his summers and winter breaks on jobsites since he was 12, Noah learned old-fashion artisanship from his father, which he combines with modern-day techniques, giving the Adelaine team an invaluably wide range of experience.

A favorite Adelaine team project was the "Leap of Faith" home on the shores of Lake Michigan. The client, who doubled as the project architect, designed the residence, which includes a main house, an eight-car garage with guest suite and an exterior living area with fieldstone fireplace and log pergola. The project evolved during construction and was one of the most exciting and exemplary projects the Adelaine team has engaged in.

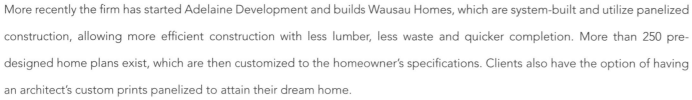

More recently the firm has started Adelaine Development and builds Wausau Homes, which are system-built and utilize panelized construction, allowing more efficient construction with less lumber, less waste and quicker completion. More than 250 pre-designed home plans exist, which are then customized to the homeowner's specifications. Clients also have the option of having an architect's custom prints panelized to attain their dream home.

With a new generation taking its place in the family business, the Little Traverse Association of Home Builders' 2007 Builder of the Year continues to expand its range of services, incorporate modern technology and remains committed to building only the highest-quality custom homes. Indeed, the future is bright for this third-generation northern Michigan builder.

ABOVE LEFT:
This 80-year-old summer cottage in Wequetonsing, Michigan was extensively remodeled, more than doubling its square footage. The stones from the fireplace were preserved and the fireplace was impeccably rebuilt.
Photograph by Dave Speckman

ABOVE RIGHT:
Natural stone and timbers were creatively assembled to form this engaging outdoor space, which was recognized in the 2007 Little Traverse Association of Home Builders Parade of Homes.
Photograph by Dave Speckman

FACING PAGE:
Natural light illuminates the dining room, exhibiting the extraordinary arched ceiling detail fashioned from clear tongue-and-groove cedar. Architecture by FAH, Inc. Harbor Springs, Michigan.
Photograph by Dave Speckman

KEVIN AKEY
FRANK ZYCHOWSKI

AZD Associates Inc.-Architects

Growing up, Kevin Akey always exercised his inherent artistic side by drawing intricate structures. But it was a chance roommate pairing with an architectural student, Frank Zychowski, AIA, at Lawrence Technological University that helped him decide where his talent would be best explored. With Frank's chosen career path as an influence, Kevin realized he could use his gift in a very dynamic way: as a residential specialist.

The former roommates collaborated in 1990, this time as partners in founding Bloomfield Hills' AZD Associates, Inc.-Architects. Today the firm has grown to comprise an award-winning team of architects and designers. Each partner balances the other's strengths dynamically: Kevin is drawn to the artistic aspects of design while Frank's expertise falls along the technical and managerial side of the profession. From Florida to California to Canada and even the Bahamas, for more than 17 years AZD has continued

ABOVE:
A combination of typical, industrial-type materials is choreographed into this maintenance-free, eco-friendly, playful residential façade.
Photograph by John Carlson, Carlson Productions

FACING PAGE:
This classic stone porte-cochère incorporates a glass floor, providing a direct visual experience with the welcoming creek below. The glass bridge is a unique twist to a truly traditional entrance.
Photograph by John Carlson, Carlson Productions

to produce livable art. Illustrating this point, the firm recently opened a satellite office in Scottsdale, Arizona, to remain responsive to its clients' regional demands.

Kevin attributes the firm's success to its detail-oriented approach with clients and impeccable reputation for delivering "edgier" designs than its more traditional mainstream counterparts. This is not to imply the firm only works in a contemporary vernacular; on the contrary, the styles they explore span Old World to traditional to contemporary and houses range from intimate lakeside residences to palatial estates. The team's innovative designs have evolved to include the use of unique materials such as hammered metals, exotic woods, structural glass and the creative implementation of masonry.

From oddly sized lake lots to unique desires of the homeowner, project diversity presents the sort of challenges the AZD design team welcomes with inventive ideas and creative aggression. Kevin asserts that they design "as much as their clients will allow." This creative freedom has led to many award-winning interiors. Most importantly, Kevin believes in bringing outdoor environments inside through the expansive use of glass. No matter the location, nature is the co-designer. However, Kevin remarks that none of these creative elements would work without proper proportion. "Perfect proportion is the key to good design, and the technical expertise that Chad Grinwis and the staff have brought to the team process adds to the equation," remarks Kevin.

The firm addresses 20 to 25 residential projects a year, yet also designs highly regarded commercial work. AZD Associates' services include interior design, custom furniture design, site supervision and fabrication of certain fixtures as well as three-dimensional renderings and computer-aided modeling.

AZD Associates' projects have been featured in many national and local publications, including *Better Homes and Gardens*, *Custom Home* and *HOUR Detroit*, and the firm has also established a presence on HGTV. The firm has been honored with more than 30 design awards, most notably, the Governor's Award for Design.

ABOVE LEFT:
The combination of glass, steel, masonry and wood defines the essence of this Prairie-style, lakefront residence.
Photograph by Christopher Lark, Christopher Lark Photography

ABOVE RIGHT:
A triangular-shaped property was the primary inspiration in developing the form of this modern, minimalist residence.
Photograph by John Carlson, Carlson Productions

FACING PAGE LEFT:
The custom-fabricated fireplace, entertainment cabinet and furniture blend seamlessly with this home's industrial-style interior.
Photograph by John Carlson, Carlson Productions

FACING PAGE RIGHT:
A covered outdoor living room extends the comfort of the interior to poolside, enhancing the experience of this classic estate.
Photograph by John Carlson, Carlson Productions

JOHN ALLEGRETTI

Allegretti Architects, Inc.

The designs of Allegretti Architects are more than just timeless structures tailored to clients' unique requirements—they represent architecture that is responsive to ecological needs and dedicated to minimizing environmental impact. At their very core, the firm's designs represent creative, organic architectural solutions that meet the owners' needs.

The son of an architect and a landscape architect, John Allegretti, FAIA, was interested in the architectural craft from his earliest beginnings. He fondly recalls pre-fabricating a small cottage with his father in their Chicago-area basement as a child. While attending the University of Arkansas, John studied under world-renowned architect Faye Jones, developing his personal understanding of the principles of organic architecture, which Jones learned from Frank Lloyd Wright before him: The idea that the smallest element becomes the reason for the largest while, conversely, the totality of the whole can be seen and embodied in the smallest part.

ABOVE LEFT:
An easterly entry and layered roof lines personify the terraced waves of water and sand, creating a gate-like shrine on the shore of Lake Michigan.
Photograph by James Yochum

ABOVE RIGHT:
Open trusses with exposed, structural insulated panels organize and provide multiple open spaces with the essential elements: shelter, heat, light, function and sense of place.
Photograph by Balthazar Korab

FACING PAGE:
This whole-house renovation and addition overlooking Lake Michigan was visually reorganized. A new façade and functionally modified plan unified and transformed the home and its architecture.
Photograph by James Yochum

John's broad perspective embraces a genuine respect for universal human values along with acute environmental sensitivity. Allegretti Architects has been designing an array of thoughtful structures comprising the built environments of the United States and Europe for the past three decades. John started Allegretti Architects in 1975, two years after OPEC's Arab oil embargo sparked an energy crisis in the United States. He designed his first solar house in 1977, and has committed his life to designing commercial, industrial and residential structures that conserve more and use less energy.

ABOVE LEFT:
A compact 2,000-square-foot home overlooking Lake Michigan presented simply in the colors of the surrounding environment welcomes one to this width-restricted site and frames the westerly views.
Photograph by James Yochum

ABOVE RIGHT:
This family weekend retreat on the shores of Lake Michigan is a metaphor for the hull of a ship and is a sterling example of the essential indoor-outdoor relationship.
Photograph by James Yochum

FACING PAGE LEFT:
A soft glow emanates from the expansive glass exterior, hinting at the rich wood ceiling and gracious spaces within.
Photograph by James Yochum

FACING PAGE RIGHT:
Curves, rectangles, triangles and squares give this home's open great room a playful yet sophisticated elegance.
Photograph by James Yochum

While certainly not every home designed by Allegretti Architects can be a solar home, John emphasizes eco-friendly design to clients via natural materials and energy-conscious, efficiently planned spaces. John holds that bigger is not always better, and designs homes that meet clients' needs while being flexible and eliminating unused space—an attempt to maximize every square foot of the home.

Allegretti Architects designs its share of luxurious residences—using sustainable resources—but the firm's true passion is forging architectural solutions that combine affordable housing design with sustainable practices in such a way that the architecture communicates back the local community's integral values. The firm has long championed the concept that remarkable architecture can take the form of socially conscious, affordable and authentically sustainable building design, thereby effecting positive change on the larger locality.

John actively gives back to his community and supports the development of architecture's next generation of practitioners, whom he encourages to carry the torch for sustainable building design. Having been recognized around the globe and having collected more than 50 design awards from the AIA, Allegretti Architects has received its share of commendation over the years, and at this point, John's firm is simply committed to one ideal: architecture that will help improve the world.

Bradford L. Angelini
Theresa L. Angelini

Angelini & Associates Architects

Brad and Theresa Angelini bring a scholarly team approach to crafting creative and appropriate architectural solutions, one that is aided by each of their invaluable design experience and manifested in their consistently inviting yet enduring architecture. Since opening Angelini & Associates Architects as a partnership in 1989, Brad and Theresa have collected a variety of awards and created designs for more than 300 projects, leaving their mark on a significant portion of Michigan's built environment.

Both Brad and Theresa earned their bachelor's degrees from Ohio State University in 1981 before obtaining a pair of master's degrees from the University of Illinois-Chicago in 1983 and Notre Dame in 1989, respectively. Brad's upbringing around the exceptional architecture of Newport, Rhode Island, developed his affinity for craftsmanship and detail, which was augmented via beneficial work experience with the firms of Holabird and Root in Chicago and César Pelli in Connecticut. He has taught architectural

ABOVE:
This renovation of a vernacular Michigan farmhouse is reminiscent of the Swedish red farmhouses depicted in the illustrations of artist Carl Larsson.
Photograph by Howard Doughty

FACING PAGE:
This showcase home extends its arms in a welcoming gesture that is accented by the trussed front porch and complemented by cedar and limestone.
Photograph by Beth Singer

design courses at the University of Michigan's College of Architecture and Urban Planning.

Theresa worked as a project architect with Allan Greenberg in Connecticut, where she was responsible for the design and construction of the Treaty Room and Diplomatic Reception Rooms in the Department of State in Washington, D.C. She also spent time working for Chicago's Hammond Beeby and Babka Architects, where she worked on the design of an addition to the Art Institute of Chicago, the Formica Showroom at the Merchandise Mart and several residential projects. Theresa has also taught architectural design courses at both the University of Michigan and Lawrence Technological University.

Working closely as a team on every project, the six-person office has established a reputation for effectively listening and communicating with clients to devise programs tailored to clients' needs and lifestyles. During the schematic design phase, the project team places an emphasis on the use of models, and will make them for anything the client wants to see—literally, whole buildings, bits and pieces of buildings, individual rooms, etc. The model-making approach provides a more comprehensive schematic than drawings, while allowing others in the office who are not involved with the project to easily offer insight. Clients can also take models home and consult with friends and family about their proposed design.

Angelini & Associates has begun to incorporate a variety of sustainable design elements into its work, and is en route to obtaining LEED certification on current and future residential projects. Using insulated concrete forms rather than traditional wood frame construction, in addition to geothermal heating and tighter, more energy-efficient designs, the firm has embraced Green design and looks to take that responsible approach to a more sophisticated level aesthetically over time.

For nearly two decades the Angelinis have cherished collaborating with clients and providing life-improving design solutions that inspire. Dedicated to advancing the principles of sound design and making a positive impact on the local community, the firm's work is reflective of its academic team approach—and will undoubtedly continue to enhance Michigan's architectural fabric for years to come.

RIGHT:
This sunken living room starts the cascade of views down the hillside beyond. The adjacent kitchen and dining room open to this room for entertaining.
Photograph by Gary Easter

FACING PAGE TOP:
An ideal location for friends and family to gather for entertaining and relaxing, this Craftsman-style kitchen has quarter-sawn oak and an oversized island.
Photograph by Howard Doughty

FACING PAGE BOTTOM:
This master bath affords private views to the surrounding woods and an interior of luxury and elegance with a glass-tiled shower and cowboy tub.
Photograph by Beth Singer

WILLIAM L. BALDNER

Clifford N. Wright Associates Architects

Clifford N. Wright began practicing architecture 60 years ago, establishing a reputation for designing exceptional residential and commercial buildings. Although Mr. Wright retired more than 20 years ago, his spirit and grand vision continue at the firm that bears his name. President William L. Baldner, AIA, joined the firm in 1977 as the architect in charge of design, and worked with Mr. Wright for eight years learning the importance of earnest client collaboration from his mentor. Bill's lasting memories of Mr. Wright include his innate ability to relate to clients, understand their goals and craft unique design solutions tailored to their specifications.

The firm has maintained its office in Bloomfield Hills since 1960, a convenient location that enables Clifford N. Wright Associates Architects to service its nearby community as well as the entire state of Michigan. Of course, with today's technology, collaborating with out-of-state clients has become a frequent reality. Recently, the firm designed a home in the Bahamas for a client in Littleton, Colorado, while working from its home office in Bloomfield Hills.

The design process for a client of Clifford N. Wright Associates Architects begins with several meetings with Bill, during which an outline of objectives, time and budget constraints, style and intended use is defined, resulting in a building program specifically fashioned for the individual.

Once the program is thoroughly understood, freehand sketches are drawn to illustrate the design. Clients appreciate the artistic, time-tested, thoughtfully crafted sketches. This is generally the first rendition of their home that they see, and Bill loves watching their faces for their initial reaction. He feels a great sense of satisfaction seeing a smile on his clients' faces—as they begin to realize the fruition of their dreams.

After the general concept is approved and carefully verified against the budget, technical drawings and specifications are formulated that convey pertinent information for construction. The freehand sketches are valued for the speed with which they can be forged, while effectively translating the spoken word to a delineated image. After the design's approval, computer-aided design plays an invaluable role in producing construction drawings that eliminate technical flaws long before ground is ever broken. Computer-generated drawings allow for the development of more complex structures with extreme accuracy. The firm takes pride in preparing coordinated technical drawings to convey the proper information to the construction trades. On numerous occasions, builders have complimented Bill on the completeness and accuracy of the firm's plans.

While Clifford N. Wright Associates Architects is certainly proud of its distinguished history and illustrious portfolio, the firm's top priority today is satisfying its current clients. They know that future opportunities are a result of today's successful projects.

Going forward, Bill sees the homes being more flexible so they can adapt to a family's changing requirements and lifestyle. Floorplans will be more open and casual to accommodate what he refers to as the "accordion effect"—families growing, shrinking and growing again as the homeowner matures. Working, professional couples without children at home will require smaller, carefree homes and will likely own two or three. Technology will allow them to live in their hometown community as well as maintain a mountain retreat, seashore cottage or northern camp. This trend will provide opportunities for CNWA beyond the state of Michigan. Homes must be more accessible and focused on sustainable design. No stranger to either barrier-free or sustainable design, Clifford N. Wright Associates Architects has incorporated these features into its designs since its inception.

As a result of the client-specific solutions that characterize the company's high level of involvement throughout the design process, Clifford N. Wright Associates Architects engages in about eight to 12 projects a year. Future commissions will likely be split between new construction and remodeling projects, both of which are equally rewarding to Bill and his staff, as they assist clients in developing their personal dream home.

RIGHT:
The architectural interior for the library in this Bloomfield Hills manor is tastefully coordinated with white oak paneling, a marble fireplace and leaded glass windows.
Photograph by Beth Singer

FACING PAGE TOP:
One of Bill's hallmarks is the skillful use of architectural columns and mouldings to define the spaces within an open floorplan while integrating interior décor.
Photograph by Jeff Garland Photography

FACING PAGE BOTTOM:
The cupola atop this Shingle-style home on historic Lake Angelus projects from the rooftop to provide extended views in all directions.
Photograph courtesy of Pella

Steven Berger
Michael Berger
Stanley Berger
Louis Beaudet

BRG Custom Homes

ABOVE:
Dramatic ceilings and expansive windows allow the beauty of the surroundings to filter into the living room.
Photograph by Beth Singer

FACING PAGE:
This Tuscan villa-style home in Bloomfield Hills uses stone accents to blend into the surrounding wooded environment.
Photograph by Beth Singer

The principals of BRG Custom Homes are a versatile team experienced in a wealth of project types. They bring invaluable knowledge and expertise to every home the company builds. The team combines this acumen with a commitment to customer service and a further commitment to crafting homes that are exceptional and fit into the landscape of the building site. The homes built by BRG are derived from clearly defined function melded with exceptional quality, timeless aesthetics and expert craftsmanship. Working in concert with the client, the team builds each home as if it were for themselves, employing rich materials and artisan labor to procure the perfect environment consistent with the unique conditions of each building site … the dream home.

Started in 1991 by Stanley Berger as a subsidiary of parent company Berger Realty Group, today BRG Custom Homes includes Stanley's sons, Michael and Steven, as well as partner Louis Beaudet. With more than two decades of commercial real estate experience, Berger Realty Group owns and manages a

portfolio of apartments, office buildings, shopping centers and industrial holdings, many of which bear the hallmarks of BRG Custom Homes' exceptional work. Offering both construction and design-build services, BRG Custom Homes has undertaken a wide range of commercial and residential projects, illustrating the versatility of this talented collective.

Whether the client purchases a condominium or a palatial estate eclipsing $2 million, the level of service, abundance of options and attention to detail remain steadfast. BRG seeks out sites with compelling characteristics—something that truly sets the site apart. Whether the location has forested views, lakefront access, rolling hills or golf course frontage, homes are designed as a part of the parcel. Spectacular sites are also often coupled with a valuable amenity, such as golf course access, country club membership or lake usage, transforming the home purchase into a true lifestyle upgrade. BRG is always highly sensitive about orienting structures to minimize effect on the landscape, save trees and promote meaningful stewardship of the environment.

Homes designed by BRG are reflective of each unique building site and community, so a wide range of styles and architecture can be found in a variety of locales—the firm largely builds in the greater metro Detroit area,

RIGHT:
Textured paint and natural brick give this study a rustic yet classic look and feel.
Photograph by Beth Singer

FACING PAGE LEFT:
The built-in bookshelves and marble fireplace invite cozy family gatherings.
Photograph by Beth Singer

FACING PAGE RIGHT:
Rich hardwood floors and French doors allow the entertaining to have an elegant feel.
Photograph by Beth Singer

including but not limited to Ann Arbor, Dundee and Ypsilanti Township. Whether a home is upscale Country French or more contemporary fit for in-town living, BRG strives to capture an Old World look with a modern bent. While each home is a unique composition, the prevalence of stone and steep rooflines—when contextually appropriate—are hallmarks of BRG's designs. A recent project led to the design of a 6,500-square-foot home exuding a farmhouse quality for a local family in Bloomfield

Township, yet the presence of modern materials like cement-board siding and a metal roof deftly blended classic design with contemporary character.

In addition to BRG's considerable single-family residential experience, they have developed numerous successful residential communities and condominium conversions. Recently, BRG developed an exciting restoration project involving the immaculate, 1920s-built Park Shelton, an architectural landmark building in downtown Detroit. This condominium conversion entailed gutting the interior, then rehabbing and restoring this gem to its original splendor. Wonderful elements such as large plaster cornices, gold-leaf paint details in the lobby, brass elevator doors and extraordinary period built-ins within units were restored and brought back to their original design.

BRG Custom Homes has collected a number of awards over the years. Steven was named the 2002 Young Builder of the Year by the Building Industry Association of Southeastern Michigan as well as 2004 Builder of the Year by the Washtenaw County Home Builders Association. A talented assemblage of experienced professionals, the team at BRG Custom Homes consistently surpasses client expectations with its commitment to quality, superior service and timeless style. In addition, the team strongly believes in giving back to the community in which it lives and works and has established a foundation, which sponsors several charitable fundraisers for the benefit of major hospitals in southeastern Michigan.

TOP RIGHT:
Stonework and architectural details surrounding the see-through fireplace add ambience and Old World charm to this home in Ann Arbor.
Photograph by Scholz Design

BOTTOM RIGHT:
Warm and welcoming, this kitchen/dinette easily becomes the gathering place for the entire family.
Photograph by Scholz Design

FACING PAGE:
This four-season room—leading to the rooftop observation terrace atop the Park Shelton—gives a formidable view of the Detroit skyline and is used for entertaining year round.
Photograph by Kevin Bauman

ALEXANDER V. BOGAERTS

Alexander V. Bogaerts + Associates

Alexander V. Bogaerts has long been passionate about design, and his affinity for architecture was originally piqued as a youth growing up in Detroit. As a first-grade student, he recalls engaging in a perspective exercise in which he laid out buildings on a city streetscape from a single-point perspective—and being completely enamored with the experience. From the planting of that design seed an exceptional career was born, and three decades of award-winning work from Alexander V. Bogaerts + Associates is a testament to the firm's extraordinary design acumen.

Upon graduation from Lawrence Technological University in Southfield, Michigan, Alexander joined a local architecture firm, becoming partner one year later and spending seven years in that role before opening his eponymous firm in 1978. The firm's work can be found throughout Michigan, all over the Midwest and in states such as California, Florida and New York. Previous projects have taken place beyond the United

States in destinations like Vacri, Italy, Ontario and Nevis Island. Providing full architectural services in both residential and commercial domains, the firm designs about six to 10 custom residences per year, ensuring that designs are of the utmost quality and attention to detail.

Growing up in Detroit's Rosedale Park, Alexander cites the superb designs of his childhood neighborhood as influential, as well as the robust Shingle-style homes of Detroit's Indian Village, a historic neighborhood comprised of architectural gems. Alexander also spent three years living in Rhode Island, and was taken with the region's vernacular, noting that "East Coast architecture is just stunning." The firm's single-family residences run the gamut from traditional to aggressively contemporary, yet all are initially derived from a strong design concept. Alexander is particularly fond of the creative freedom and wide-open palette that modern designs afford, but he also delights in designing in more traditional vocabularies such as French Country or Shingle style with their rich details and longstanding nuances.

TOP LEFT:
A variety of prominent gable rooflines establishes a pleasant rhythm across this lakefront façade. Projecting east and west porches frame this Shingle-style home.
Photograph by Alexander V. Bogaerts + Associates

BOTTOM LEFT:
A commanding front entry detail sets the design theme for this classical home. A significant landscape walkway edge reinforces the importance of the home's welcoming door.
Photograph courtesy of Alexander V. Bogaerts + Associates

FACING PAGE TOP:
Dramatic façade offsets create the basis for a powerful European-style exterior. Accented rooflines above the second-floor windows add scale and interest to complete a balanced exterior.
Photograph by Alexander V. Bogaerts + Associates

FACING PAGE BOTTOM:
Complementary crescent and wave architectural forms command this contemporary lakefront home. The extensive use of glass railings allows uninterrupted water views.
Photograph by Balthazar Korab

Homes designed by Alexander V. Bogaerts + Associates represent an integral response to the project site and the achievement of the homeowner's hopes and dreams for the residence. The resultant design is the careful coalescence of those imperative qualities via a well-conceived, captivating architectural statement in response to those pertinent needs. One such home was built entirely on designated wetlands, and the completed project achieved the homeowner's desires in a compelling home while preserving the environmental quality of a sensitive site.

After 30 years of industry success, Alexander V. Bogaerts + Associates will continue to design enduring architectural solutions throughout the country and beyond, and place an even greater emphasis on sustainable design and building—a recent five-story residential project designed by the firm is entirely geothermal. Dedicated to consistent design excellence, Alexander tells clients, "this is your home, but it's my house forever." It is this undying commitment to superior quality that defines the work of this venerable firm.

JOHN CHOATE

Choate Custom Homes, LLC
Choate Custom Design

Truly building a dream home is an exercise in customization. While any newly built house is functional and provides shelter, a house does not become a home without an owner's personal touches. From the flow of a house to its materials, accessories and spaces, any homeowner's ideal residence is the synthesis of these and other choices, fully tailored to unique needs and desires. Clients who collaborate with Choate Custom Homes rest assured that any desire—no matter how grandiose or whimsical—can and will be incorporated into their new dream home.

John Choate has been around building and all kinds of construction his entire life. From the early days as a youth assisting his father as the family repairman—and in a family with seven kids, there were plenty of repairs to be made—to his adolescent jobs working on jobsites, pouring concrete and working for a brick mason. By the time he built his first house in 1985, there were no aspects involved with construction or building homes that he had not already done before. His firm, Choate Custom Homes, has been designing

ABOVE:
This foyer welcomes guests with warm walnut flooring, a mix of stained and painted hardwoods and a wood barrel ceiling.
Photograph by Beth Singer

FACING PAGE:
This custom Cape Cod home was built on a five-acre estate lot to provide the owners with plenty of privacy and room to enjoy their greenhouse gardens and carriage house, which protects their collector automobiles.
Photograph by Beth Singer

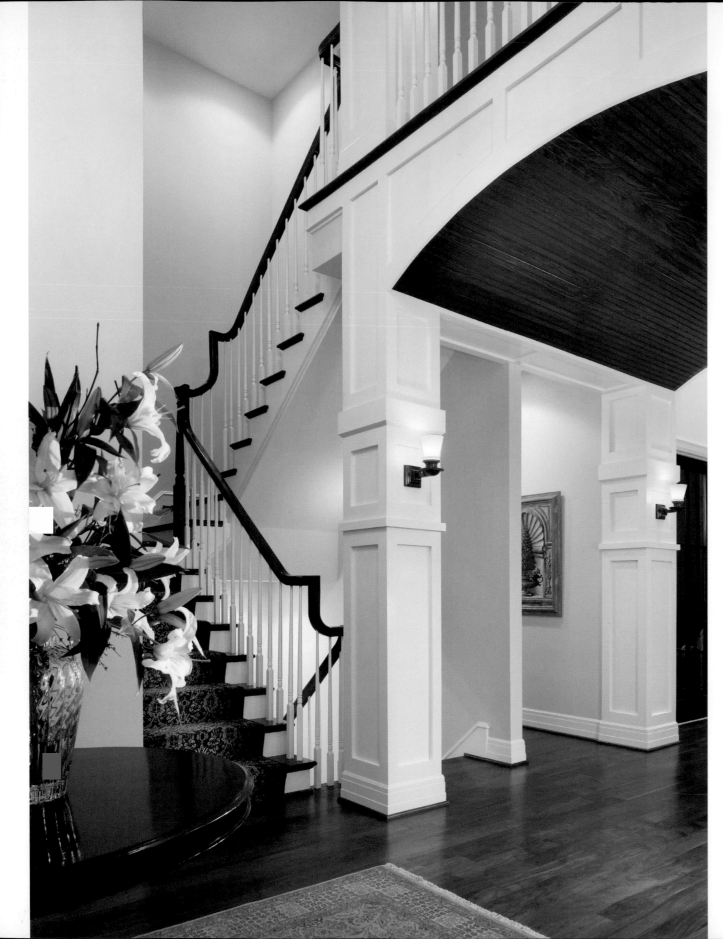

and building bona fide custom homes for the past 20 years, combining his vast experience with literally myriad design options, ensuring 100-percent customer satisfaction on every project it undertakes.

Choate Custom Homes begins the homebuilding process with its distinct LifeCentric™ System, a thorough process of ascertaining each family or potential homeowner's lifestyle to assist the Choate team in crafting a home that not only fits but enhances his or her life. This well-refined system has long been utilized by the firm, and provides an ideal foundation for designing a one-of-a-kind home, identifying any type of need down to the smallest detail so that the Choate team can implement features into the homes that fit clients' lives.

Moreover, the firm and their partner architects use advanced computer-generated virtual design software to allow homeowners to virtually walk through and around their home before construction ever commences. In addition to helping clients envision their homes, a task often found

LEFT:
Quiet elegance was achieved with these Cape Cod-style stairs as the owner did not want them seen as a major focal point upon entering the home.
Photograph by Beth Singer

FACING PAGE LEFT:
The goal for this kitchen was to design a comfortable and functional workspace for a casual gourmet chef.
Photograph by Beth Singer

FACING PAGE RIGHT:
Dry-stacked Jerusalem stone was utilized to create a two-story fireplace of interest in this wood-paneled study.
Photograph by Beth Singer

difficult via traditional, two-dimensional blueprints, the software enables them to pinpoint unwanted design aspects and make changes in a significantly less-costly manner. As well, Choate Custom Design, a separate entity unto itself, offers the ability to shop, design and seamlessly coordinate materials and finishes. Collectively, these various services allow customers to handle all their design-build needs from the same entity, simplifying the building experience. All clients also receive a personal user name and password, allowing them to log into the firm's website and check on their home's status 24 hours a day.

Choate Custom Homes builds homes from 3,500 square feet to more than 20,000 square feet and in any and all styles, from traditional Mediterranean, Country French and Italianate to ultra contemporary, and any request is attainable. Past Choate homeowners have requested such extraordinary features as a 40-foot by 20-foot by 8-foot saltwater tank used to house full-size black tip sharks, providing them with ample room to swim and circle around. Other novelty home features have included dog showers, specialty doghouses under staircases and a prayer room with a temple that provided its homeowners with an intimate space for meditation. One client in Pinckney, Michigan, had a home in progress, already framed, when she decided she wanted to have a fourth floor on what was being built as a three-story house. Thus, the design team went back to the drawing boards; designed and engineered a way to give her a fourth floor; cut off the roof that had just been put on; redesigned that space and reconfigured some of the floor structure; and finally built a spiral staircase to give her a fourth floor. Needless to say, the client was delighted with the result, which essentially gave her a fourth-floor observatory, as that space was nearly 50 feet high in her home.

Combining John Choate's all-encompassing construction knowledge with a systematic process that uncovers the minutiae of every client's day-to-day lifestyle, Choate Custom Homes designs and builds wholly customized residences with any imaginable feature—guaranteeing 100-percent customer satisfaction each and every time.

RIGHT:
This foyer's freestanding iron spiral staircase was designed to capture the attention of visitors as they enter the home.
Photograph by Beth Singer

FACING PAGE LEFT:
To satisfy the homeowner's love of art and fine woodwork this study was designed and painted to provide a semblance of works by the owner's favorite artist Michelangelo and his *Creation of Man*.
Photograph by Beth Singer

FACING PAGE RIGHT:
Emulation of an Old World French pub/game room was the design goal for this bar, in which the ceilings are pressed copper tiles and the signage is authentic French paraphernalia.
Photograph by Beth Singer

ROBERT CLARKE

CBi Design Professionals, Inc.

ABOVE:
This rural Romeo home is the signature home in a private development. The design focuses views in all directions, overlooking nature preserves, ponds and long vistas regularly home to a wide variety of wildlife.
Photograph by Beth Singer

FACING PAGE:
This Upper Straights lakefront home maximizes long views to the rear with a rural estate façade toward a large motor court on the street. Indiana limestone columns, water table base courses and quoins are mixed with brick detailing and wood shingle roof.
Photograph by Beth Singer

When potential clients meet architect Robert Clarke, AIA, they know immediately that this is one architect who is truly committed to assisting them in accomplishing their dream home, whether by original design or exceptional renovation. Perhaps this knowledge comes in light of the history of Robert Clarke's career, determination and success; or perhaps it is because he designs his homes and additions with a realistic construction process in mind—or a combination of those facts and much more.

Growing up in the rural Michigan town of Cass City, Robert's father, a high school agriculture teacher, encouraged his son's interest in architecture and construction. To that end, his parents even purchased a fire-damaged home, which Robert renovated and rebuilt over one and half years for credit in a high school co-operative program. Nearly 30 years later, his parents still own the home.

While earning his two degrees at Lawrence Technological University, in 1985 Robert secured a position as a draftsman for a developer and builder of custom single-family homes, Bruce E. Bordener & Associates. Within two short years he was head of the 10-person architectural outgrowth sector of the company. Determined that dynamic architectural designs could broaden the practice, by 1989 a separate company was formed with the help of Mr. Bordener. Accordingly, Robert became president before the age of 30 and sole owner by 1996, at which time the company's name was changed to CBi Design Professionals.

Today, as always, the firm's talented team of professionals, led by Robert, is dedicated to providing its clients with the highest-quality design solutions in the built environment. Though many design firms tend to shy away from the often-challenging conditions of renovation and rehabilitation work, CBi invites these opportunities to discover new solutions. Motivated by his design philosophies, Robert focuses his practice on attention to detail, client service and site considerations of luxury single-family homes, renovations and additions. Although Robert appreciates the recognition of his work, his goal is to ensure that CBi's additions appear as if they were original to the structure and that the building has just been meticulously maintained over the years. CBi's primary projects are residentially based and in the traditional vernacular, although, with no design boundaries, the firm has addressed religious and light commercial projects as well.

The recipient of many design awards for renovations and new residences—from such sources as *Detroit Home Magazine*, *Professional Builder & Remodeling Magazine* and *Metropolitan Detroit Home*, to name a few—CBi Design Professionals' diversification in the architectural sector under Robert's leadership is a credit to his continual design quality and the uniqueness of his work.

TOP RIGHT:
This Italian-style farmhouse outside of Mason was renovated and dramatically expanded to recapture the original charm that had been lost through years of poorly designed additions and aluminum cladding. The garage and farm buildings were brought up to an estate level to round out a beautiful home.
Photograph by Beth Singer

BOTTOM RIGHT:
This Lake Michigan resort home rests at the edge of protected sand dunes and captures views down the shipping lanes through the straits of Mackinaw. The owners wanted a blend between a lake cottage for her and stone castle for him with large windows to view the lake, making this a truly challenging but unique style.
Photograph by Beth Singer

FACING PAGE LEFT:
The library is part of a full octagonal tower overlooking water features and a private nature preserve. The design is reminiscent of the old auto-baron residences from the early 20th century.
Photograph by Beth Singer

FACING PAGE RIGHT:
This breakfast space, with a kitchen and hearth room, is an integral part of the family activity area yet maintains its own individuality. The space overlooks a beautiful rear yard and pool, making it the focal point of activity.
Photograph by Beth Singer

Louis DesRosiers

DesRosiers Architects

After more than 35 years in the profession and being a third-generation architect, Lou DesRosiers still possesses the unbridled enthusiasm and appetite for creativity as if it were his first year. His affinity for design is no doubt a family heirloom, but so is his faculty for playing the piano. This duet of artistic talents has prompted his characterization of architecture as frozen music. Song has form, function, undulations, contrast and harmony—architecture shares these attributes, and when done masterfully comes together as a three-dimensional symphony. True of any artist, Lou is constantly seeking new ways to perfect his craft and is constantly pushing the envelope of design.

Lou has literally had a lifetime of education in architecture, following the lead of his father Arthur DesRosiers, who in 1930 designed the nationally award-winning St. Hugo's of the Hills Church in Bloomfield Hills, Michigan. As a youth, drawing came naturally to him. He refined his skills in ensuing years, earning

ABOVE:
Reflective of a five-diamond resort boutique, this dramatic pool and terrace complement the Asian flair of the Wrightian architecture.
Photograph by George Dzahristos

FACING PAGE:
The striking, cantilevered portico protrudes from the roofline and is a dramatic focal point of the Prairie-styled residence. Indigenous materials such as mahogany, cedar and Fon du Lac sprawl across the landscape.
Photograph by George Dzahristos

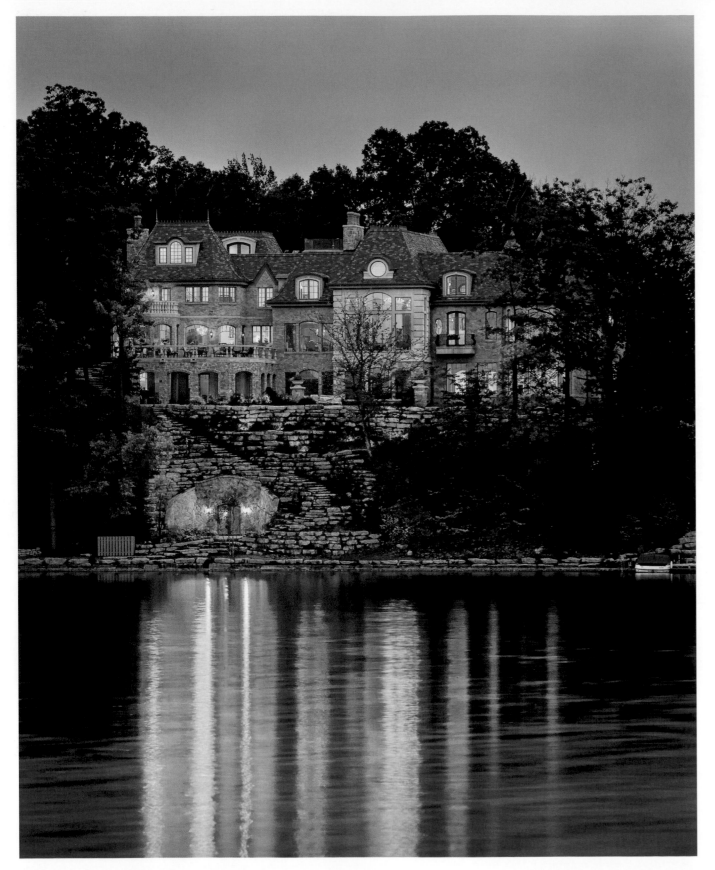

highest honors in Lawrence Technological University's design curriculum, and became a registered architect in 1976. As a young practitioner, Lou designed and built his first home in 1972 in rural Michigan, an invaluable experience that he credits as the launch of his residential career. His upbringing consisted of many construction tasks alongside his father, but designing and building this sophisticated, contemporary 6,000-square-foot home allowed him to engage in every detail of the process. Moreover, for a young architect, the house served as an impressive, full-scale portfolio for prospective clients, leading to one of his first major projects.

Since opening his firm, DesRosiers Architects, more than three decades ago, Lou has been dedicated to creating remarkable designs that delight homeowners upon every return. This has been accomplished via an expansive collection of designs divided into three main categories: traditional, contemporary and Shingle styles. The firm's traditional homes range from French Renaissance to Colonial while contemporary offerings are influenced by everything from the Wrightian to the postmodern. DesRosiers Architects is well known for designing around bodies of water, and its unique Great Lakes style is found in homes dotting Michigan shorelines. These homes are inspired by Atlantic Shingle style, which first appeared in New York vacation dwellings lining the Atlantic Coast in the 1890s featuring a cedar shake and stone palette.

Whatever the style, specific design philosophies transcend each of the firm's residences, namely: the prevalence of open spaces, a profusion of natural light and sculptural-quality aesthetics. Designing easily accessible spaces that flow seamlessly from one to another is a pertinent aspect of every DesRosiers home. The use of abundant natural light in the firm's

designs stems from Lou's affinity for the outdoors and near-obsession of providing the perfect view. This is a surprising contrast from his childhood home. Built in 1930 by his father, Arthur, it was a beautiful French Norman house, characterized by heavy walls and abundant masonry where windows were more of an accent than a feature.

ABOVE:
The informal gathering room affords breathtaking views of Lake Michigan.
Photograph by Bruce Buck

RIGHT:
The grand columns on this award-winning vacation home suggest pavilions of the past.
Photograph by Glen Rauth

FACING PAGE:
Reminiscent of a French chateau, this stately 15,000-square-foot home on Upper Straits Lake exudes an air of mystery and romance. A roof patio-to-tunnel elevator affords quick access to the lake and its splendor.
Photograph by Beth Singer

The details are what distinguish a DesRosiers home. Staircases are often spiral sculptures showcased and on display in the foyer. Composed of glass and mysteriously suspended, they become a focal point for all to admire. The artistry continues with cleverly concealed air vents, electrical outlets and even exterior gutters. Constantly pursuing new ideas, Lou has created and routinely implements a number of inventive techniques, which have become his trademark. Elevators, roof patios, tunnels, lighthouses and rooftop spas and fire pits are just a few of the cutting-edge amenities found in his homes.

With an insatiable passion for architecture, Lou approaches the future with the same fervor as when he entered the profession. He is constantly seeking projects that challenge his abilities along with the boundaries of design. One of the firm's latest opportunities to do so is with a 20-acre family estate on Martha's Vineyard. DesRosiers Architects will be sure to form yet another masterpiece.

RIGHT:
The exquisite architecture in the dining room was designed to showcase an extensive collection of Far East treasures.
Photograph by Beth Singer

FACING PAGE LEFT:
Bands of contrasting smooth limestone and split-face Fon du Lac establish the massive module of this 8,000-square-foot contemporary home. Floor-to-ceiling glass in the cantilevered living room offers 125-foot, panoramic lake views.
Photograph by George Dzahristos

FACING PAGE RIGHT:
This spectacular foyer leads to the dramatic great room. A floating ceiling allows morning light to enter through clerestory windows. Textured mountain green granite pillars offset mahogany wood walls.
Photograph by George Dzahristos

ABOVE LEFT:
Large expanses of glass let the interior glow reflect onto the outdoor pool at this resort-like residence located on an inland lake.
Photograph by Laszlo Regos

ABOVE RIGHT:
The helical staircase serves as a sculptural centerpiece of the entrance rotunda.
Photograph by Laszlo Regos

ABOVE:
Illuminated columns are mirrored in the inviting waters of the indoor pool and spa.
Photograph by Laszlo Regos

MARTY EASLING

Easling Construction

Providing more than 30 years of continuous service in Leelanau and Grand Traverse counties, Easling Construction is a premier builder in northern lower Michigan. Adept at all aspects of construction, Marty Easling simply knows high-quality construction. Growing up in Grand Traverse County as the son of an engineer who was the vice president of a construction company, Marty was immersed in building from his beginnings and naturally followed in his father's footsteps. Since starting Easling Construction in 1976, Marty has established lasting customer relationships, grown and refined his enterprise and now oversees a 100-plus-person operation that is simply unmatched in quality, experience and service among builders in the area.

After graduating from Michigan Technological University with a Bachelor of Science in civil engineering, Marty returned to his hometown where he preferred to live, and worked as an engineer for a highway construction firm. Two years later, wanting to be challenged more and build buildings, Marty started

ABOVE:
Simple painted trim and detail are reflected in this tasteful yet elegant guest bedroom bath.
Photograph by Peter Tata

FACING PAGE:
This Shingle-style home in Empire, Michigan, commands a spectacular panoramic view of Lake Michigan from all primary living spaces. Architecture by Robert L. Holdeman, AAI, Inc.
Photograph by Peter Tata

Easling Construction. Two years later he purchased another construction company. Since merging the two entities, Easling Construction has grown swiftly over the years, and today includes seven foremen with crews that work year round. Located near Leland, the firm has undertaken a wide array of commercial and residential projects throughout northwestern lower Michigan and is well-equipped to provide services for any construction project. Clients also benefit from knowing that Marty visits virtually every job site every day, lending credence to the notion of a truly hands-on principal.

Engaging in projects small and large, Easling Construction has built hundreds of homes in the Leland and Grand Traverse areas—as well as churches, restaurants, office buildings and condominiums—and is dedicated to providing superior service in northwestern lower Michigan. Marty is a firm believer that handling as much work as possible in-house is

TOP LEFT:
The great room with cathedral ceilings and heavy timber trusses provides immediate and commanding views of Lake Michigan, fostering an integral indoor-outdoor relationship.
Photograph by Peter Tata

BOTTOM LEFT:
The plan of the entry court was dictated by site constraints and spatial relationships. Paving materials were introduced to provide a warm welcoming to both owner and guests.
Photograph by Peter Tata

FACING PAGE LEFT:
Self-watering flower boxes keep an abundance of color fresh and fragrant all summer.
Photograph by Eric J. Smith

FACING PAGE RIGHT:
The main interior and exterior rooms of the home overlook Lake Michigan, providing resplendent vistas throughout the home.
Photograph by Eric J. Smith

essential, as it allows for efficient, more tightly controlled schedules and ensures consistent, first-rate quality. After all, what homeowner wouldn't rather have a custom-made home over factory-produced? Moreover, Marty employs some of the most talented craftsmen in his part of the state, and his skilled tradespeople genuinely enjoy the customization and artisan-style detailing of the firm's work.

Indeed, homes built by Easling Construction contain craftsmanship of the utmost quality. The in-house skilled staff regularly engages in its own concrete, masonry, rough and finish carpentry, insulation, roofing, drywall hanging and finishing, hardwood floors, ceramic tile, cabinetry and painting. The firm's millwork shop encompasses more than 5,500 square feet and is home to a variety of equipment run by three year-round employees, enabling the firm to do any custom work it needs with speed and precision.

RIGHT:
The upper book gallery overlooks the living and dining areas and is warmed by the prevalence of various natural woods.
Photograph by Eric J. Smith

FACING PAGE LEFT:
Handmade tiles complement the custom-built cabinetry by Easling's millshop.
Photograph by Eric J. Smith

FACING PAGE CENTER:
Freestanding plumbing fixtures provide interest in this bathroom.
Photograph by Eric J. Smith

FACING PAGE RIGHT:
Opening out to the terrace, this room features wall paneling crafted from 150-year-old white pine.
Photograph by Eric J. Smith

Because of northern Michigan's especially cold winters, the vast majority of homes built by Easling Construction are vacation homes that are occupied seasonally. So naturally, when homeowners are out of town, no one is there to maintain their residences. Easling Construction offers a variety of home maintenance services, helping to ensure that the substantial investment made by the homeowner is protected well into the future. Available maintenance services include snow plowing, window washing, house cleaning, pressure washing, painting and touch-ups, house visits and inspections, home repairs and monitoring services.

As a trained civil engineer with a lifetime's worth of building experience, Marty truly cherishes the challenge of taking an architect's one-of-a-kind design and making it work. Easling Construction has worked with a number of architects from near and far—past designs have come from architects based in New York, Chicago, Detroit, Columbus and, of course, northwestern lower Michigan—whose designs range from Old World to contemporary and take an array of forms.

LEFT:
The warmth of the northern Michigan experience is reflected in the American cherry cabinetry and detail in this Traverse City condominium. Architecture by Robert L. Holdeman, AAI, Inc., Interior architecture by Scott Lankford, Lankford Design Group.
Photograph by Peter Tata

FACING PAGE TOP:
Cherry paneling and detailing are carried throughout the condominium's master bedroom. Subtle lighting provides the appropriate ambience.
Photograph by Peter Tata

FACING PAGE BOTTOM:
The open plan of the living, dining and gallery spaces reflects the inviting, contemporary northern Michigan expression.
Photograph by Peter Tata

Providing service throughout Leelanau and Grand Traverse counties since 1976, Easling Construction has built outstanding rapport with an ever-growing list of satisfied clientele in a market where referrals, repeat business and positive word-of-mouth are essential. Dedicated to consistently providing only first-rate service, Marty brings a hands-on approach to projects that is rendered invaluable thanks to his copious construction knowledge. His team of skilled in-house tradespeople and selected subcontractors ensures consistently exceptional quality, making Easling Construction a premier builder in northern lower Michigan.

TIM FISHER

Indesign, Inc.

Based in the small and beautiful town of Charlevoix for more than 25 years, Indesign has worked with its clients to provide compelling, highly detailed design and quality craftsmanship on projects—not only throughout Michigan but nationwide, with recently completed projects in Florida, Ohio, Indiana and a spectacular penthouse in downtown Chicago.

Indesign is unique in that it is a collection of talented architects, interior designers, kitchen and bath experts, lighting designers, furniture and fabric professionals, along with surface and material specialists, all under one roof to provide smooth interaction throughout the design and development process. While a client may not enlist all of these skilled trades on any one particular project, access to this cadre of experienced professionals ensures an ideal fit for whatever type of project the client may have.

ABOVE:
The interior entrance of this Charlevoix home offers views across the inlaid marble floor to the dining room, up the sweeping grand staircase to the guestrooms and into the great room. Design by Indesign, Inc.
Photograph by Phoenix Photographic Studio

FACING PAGE:
This Charlevoix home overlooking Lake Michigan is an exquisite rendition of a European stone mansion—majestic in every way. Architecture by H. Jack Begrow, AIA, in collaboration with Indesign, Inc.
Photograph by Phoenix Photographic Studio

Though clients can select their own builder, the firm has a great collection of builder referrals. These tried-and-true builders value the seamless communication the Indesign team facilitates between the client and workers on site. The firm has also worked with many talented architects throughout the country, bringing synergy and complementary talents to such projects.

The firm's designs further represent the aspirations and personalities of its clients. This approach to architecture and interior design is a partnership between the client and project team. Indesign is committed to maintaining architectural integrity while creating exceptional design rich in architectural elements that are both practical and timeless. The team's inspiration is often guided by historical precedent and the desire to capture the romance of a particular place.

Architecture is the highest form of collaboration, integrating the needs and dreams of the client. At the end of the project, clients continuously comment on how valuable the team approach was for

them and how their ideas were transformed with great efficiency. Indesign has gained an impeccable reputation for responsive service and innovative design, and has developed a strong bond with its clients/friends by working with them not only on original projects but with ongoing additions and remodels as well. The firm has built its business through delighted clients and their direct referrals.

The size and scale of projects vary from small remodel projects to grand, full-scale endeavors. Of course, all projects, no matter the size, benefit from good design, and the best design comes from the combined talents of a team. Indesign undertakes projects in a wide range of styles and sizes, and cherishes the challenge of working with any style that its clients desire. Those styles range anywhere from Shingle-style, French Country or English cottage to full log home, applied half-log, Prairie-style or contemporary.

The Indesign team takes the time to meet with clients and listen to their every need to develop a program that is ideally suited to their tastes. Indesign has, over the years, developed a comfortable meeting format that will maximize clients' time and speed the design process along. During the design process, both interior and exterior design perspectives are developed to help the client better visualize how the completed project will look. An integral project element is working with an interior designer while simultaneously developing the architectural design. It is very important

ABOVE LEFT:
This great room exudes an extraordinary level of detail, which is prevalent throughout the magnificent home, particularly in the inlaid floors, grand fireplace and unique stair details. Design by Indesign, Inc.
Photograph by Phoenix Photographic Studio

ABOVE RIGHT:
The carved bar and immaculate island support posts are in harmony with the large custom range hood, set on a jarrah-and-slate inlaid floor. The floor and ceiling grid unify the space. Design by Indesign, Inc.
Photograph by Phoenix Photographic Studio

FACING PAGE:
This Shingle-style manor features an expansive use of glass, allowing full vantage of the spectacular Lake Charlevoix vistas. The manor is surrounded by a flowing creek, weaving its way through the incredible landscaping. Architecture by N.J. White, AIA, in collaboration with Indesign, Inc. Constructed by Ed Bajos.
Photograph by Phoenix Photographic Studio

to develop the furniture layout and true uses of the home along with good kitchen and bath design early on in the process. Critical mistakes can be eliminated when fusing these talents.

Additional pertinent elements of exceptional design are the review and consideration of lighting, audio/video, color coordination, surface and materials, furniture and fabrics, and landscape architecture. During the construction phase, the firm continues to oversee the project to assure that the plans are followed, the specifications are met and that the job is progressing on schedule and on budget.

Indesign's work is about taking people's ideas and translating them into residential and commercial showplaces by leading clients through the evolution of design. The firm strives to consistently produce creative solutions: delivering designs that meet and exceed clients' expectations continues to distinguish the multitalented Indesign team.

ABOVE:
The log and Shingle-style lodge is captivating for its rich material palette and craftsmanship. This lakeside view exhibits the expansive use of glass to take full advantage of the resplendent Lake Charlevoix views. Architecture by H. Jack Begrow, AIA, in collaboration with Indesign Inc. Constructed by Ray Wallick.
Photograph by Phoenix Photographic Studio

FACING PAGE LEFT:
This grand lodge overlooking Lake Charlevoix is spacious yet warmed by its material and color selections, as well as the flow from the great room through the dining room and out into the large octagonal porch with stone fireplace. Design by Indesign, Inc.
Photograph by Phoenix Photographic Studio

FACING PAGE RIGHT:
This lower-level game room includes a large octagonal bar, behind which comfortable seating and a grand fireplace offer an ideal space for leisure. The entrance guard is a spectacular elk mount. Design by Indesign, Inc.
Photograph by Phoenix Photographic Studio

KEVIN HART

Kevin Hart Associates

From his beginnings in Detroit and early awe-inspiring childhood visits to the renowned Cranbrook Institute in Bloomfield Hills, Kevin Hart, AIA, has long enjoyed a passion for exceptional design. Over the years Kevin has delved into a multitude of design and engineering endeavors, and today leads an artistic, comprehensive team at Kevin Hart Associates, a firm wholly committed to design excellence.

Kevin refined his knowledge and cultivated his design passion at the University of Notre Dame, where he majored in architectural engineering and was also a member of the university's 1977 national championship football team. He launched his architecture and design firm in 1990 and today works intimately with clients, along with senior designer Patty Keller, project designer Leslie Ingersoll and talented local interior designer Julia Knevels to provide consistently compelling architectural solutions.

ABOVE:
Subtle detailing and soft colors provide an inviting entryway.
Photograph by Kastler Construction

FACING PAGE:
This romantic Norman Tudor has soft, natural materials and classic detailing. Richly appointed terraces with swooping rooflines feature bluestone paving and authentic timber woodwork.
Photograph by Pam and Dan Maresca

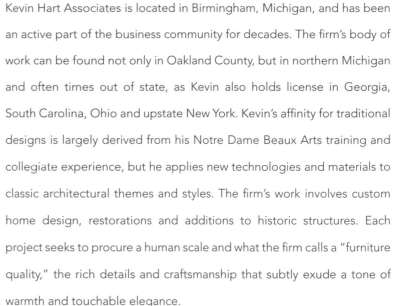

Kevin Hart Associates is located in Birmingham, Michigan, and has been an active part of the business community for decades. The firm's body of work can be found not only in Oakland County, but in northern Michigan and often times out of state, as Kevin also holds license in Georgia, South Carolina, Ohio and upstate New York. Kevin's affinity for traditional designs is largely derived from his Notre Dame Beaux Arts training and collegiate experience, but he applies new technologies and materials to classic architectural themes and styles. The firm's work involves custom home design, restorations and additions to historic structures. Each project seeks to procure a human scale and what the firm calls a "furniture quality," the rich details and craftsmanship that subtly exude a tone of warmth and touchable elegance.

Patty Keller has been with Kevin and the firm from the onset, and brings more than 20 years of experience in the architectural and historical fields. Her expertise in design and adaptive-use issues provides a unique and creative approach to every project. After establishing client relationships, Patty helps guide all aspects of residential and commercial projects

TOP LEFT:
The open floorplan has a traditional flavor with defined spaces enhanced by pronounced millwork and dramatic archways.
Photograph by Kastler Construction

BOTTOM LEFT:
Historically true elements give this New England colonial a timeless feel. Recycled blast-furnace brick and sustainable construction materials were selected to provide beauty and durability for generations to come.
Photograph by Pam and Dan Maresca

FACING PAGE TOP:
The contemporary geometry of this home illustrates the drama and character of Prairie School design.
Photograph by Lynn Helm

FACING PAGE BOTTOM:
This Georgian residence features the proportion and symmetry of a bygone era. Highly detailed mouldings and siding are comprised of durable composite material.
Photograph by Pam and Dan Maresca

from design to final construction. Her pride in historical accuracy and proportional detail combine with vision and function to produce award-winning designs.

The firm's team approach provides clients with multiple viewpoints on design decisions, and Kevin and Patty will hand draw their ideas during initial meetings. This inclusive approach allows the client to easily relate to concepts and even pick up a pencil to help guide the design interpretation. An exciting current project involves the design of new yet historically accurate structures on Laurel Island in Georgia, where capacity requirements and modern systems must be delicately balanced with an engaging scale and classic aesthetics. This particular Old Country design will feature geothermal heating and cooling, low-emission lighting and the use of recycled materials. The island project has a wonderful spirit of stewardship and represents the responsible development of a pristine coastal community rich in heritage and tradition.

Kevin Hart Associates has garnered seven design awards from *HOUR Detroit* and *Detroit Home Magazine* and was featured in *Better Homes and Gardens*. While many commissions are taking root outside of the Great Lakes State, the firm is earnestly committed to Michigan's rich tradition, consistently providing exceptional design, planning and engineering services to satisfied clientele.

MICHAEL R. KLEMENT

Architectural Resource

Architecture: the art and science of designing and erecting buildings. Resource: a source of supply, support or aid; especially one that can be readily drawn upon when needed or required. Architectural Resource: a collective of outstanding, talented individuals, passionately committed to providing design expertise and crafting intimately tailored, exquisite architectural solutions that both endure and delight.

As principal of Ann Arbor's Architectural Resource, Michael Klement, AIA, has long held that the home is the platform from which to stage one's life. The talented team of professionals at Architectural Resource consistently solves clients' design challenges in ways that generate inspiring arenas from which their clients lead enhanced lives. Engaging exclusively in residential work, the vast majority of which encompasses renovations, remodels and additions, the firm has completed inspired projects throughout southeastern Michigan as well as beyond the Great Lakes State.

Michael posits that every great project first begins with a great client. He emphasizes that the initial stages of design are the most critical in ensuring a project's ultimate success; "To get the best answers, one needs to ask the best questions, both of the client and of the existing context, whether an unbuilt site or an existing home." This dialogue is essential to solving the clients' design challenges through their own unique perspective. Architectural Resource employs a rigorous and thorough discovery and design methodology that is key to avoiding missed opportunities and eliminating errors and surprises later in the process. The firm's unique, proprietary approach elucidates the client's optimal design solutions via a systematic process that continually clarifies goals, opportunities and challenges for both the architect and the client.

TOP RIGHT:
This Arts-and-Crafts-style bungalow renovation presents a warm gathering space with Mowtawi tile, custom woodwork and stained glass handcrafted by the homeowner.
Photograph by Stanley Livingston

BOTTOM LEFT:
Dining at home has a whole new ambience thanks to this new daily dining inglenook with custom, client-specific ergonomics.
Photograph by Stanley Livingston

BOTTOM RIGHT:
Rich craftsmanship is evident in the clustered and cross-tied column design motif carried through the entire project.
Photograph by Stanley Livingston

FACING PAGE:
This Arts-and-Crafts bungalow was entirely renovated, including a rebuilt front porch, kitchen bay extension and 200-square-foot addition at rear. Built by Washtenaw Woodwrights.
Photograph by Stanley Livingston

While every remodel project completed by Architectural Resource is a one-of-a-kind transformation derived from each client's unique outlook, it is also a deft marriage of old and new. Sensitively relating the remodeled design to its original form, revitalized homes appear as though their impeccable design had always existed as a unified, harmonious composition. A recent project in southeastern Michigan challenged Architectural Resource to remodel a home with the primary goal of creating an architectural event, a sculptural, one-of-a-kind fireplace that would be the focal point of a room offering leisure space and access to an exterior deck. The home was contemporary yet rustic, characterized by angled, projecting gable forms and soaring sheets of glass. One of the home's exterior features included a pattern of stacked and staggered two-by-two windows, a motif repeated throughout the house.

LEFT:
This sunroom addition showcases precisely detailed and executed moulding, trim and paneling with featured Andersen Art glass accent. Built by Custom Construction.
Photograph by Susan Webb

FACING PAGE LEFT:
This contemporary interior remodel introduced a minimalist sculptural fireplace and natural light to a mundane, highly shaded 1950s' ranch home. Built by Custom Construction.
Photograph by Stanley Livingston

FACING PAGE RIGHT:
This historically sensitive, classic conservatory addition to an 1800s' Italianate landmark residence replaced a deteriorating side porch. Built by Home Renewal.
Photograph by Stanley Livingston

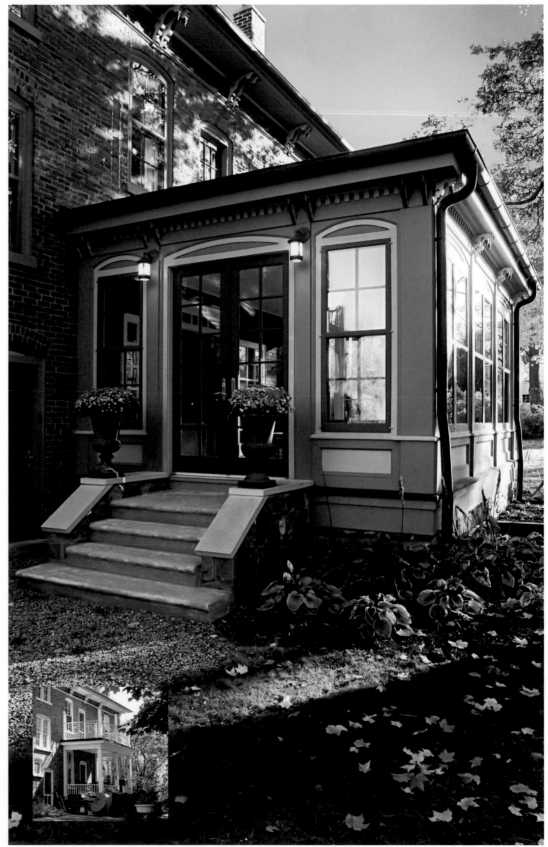

Architectural Resource's design solution created a stunning centerpiece fireplace—a unique composition of metal, concrete and plaster—that echoed the gables' angled forms in the fireplace's cantilevered mantel, projecting hearth and a rectilinear pattern in the elegant stone floor. The staggered-window theme was reinterpreted and brought into the addition through a skylight array above the fireplace that created an evolving pattern of light as the backdrop to this sculptural element. The space is defined by warmth from the stained wood ceiling and stone tile floor and set against a serene outdoor backdrop thoughtfully brought inside via the expansive fenestration—all of which centered on the sublime fireplace evoking the form of the home's captivating, outward-thrusting gables.

ABOVE LEFT:
This contemporary addition showcases a custom-fabricated, projecting metal fireplace mantel and cast concrete hearth extension.
Photograph by James Haefner

ABOVE CENTER:
The mantel brackets have custom vases and supports. Materials and finishes designed by Paul Hickman.
Photograph by James Haefner

ABOVE RIGHT:
An evening view of this contemporary addition illustrates the stacked and staggered skylight array interpretation of the existing window motif.
Photograph by James Haefner

FACING PAGE:
This contemporary addition's massing and thrusting, gabled roof forms echo those of the existing home. Built by Mark Dennis.
Photograph by James Haefner

A hallmark of Architectural Resource's philosophy is promoting ecological responsibility via sustainable building practices. The firm has long championed energy-efficient buildings and Green design. Energy efficiency was part of Michael's core curriculum during his studies at the University of Michigan, and Architectural Resource is eager to embrace sustainable design to the level with which its clients are comfortable. The firm employs U.S. Green Building Council LEED-accredited professionals within the office. Michael's participation in numerous organizations dedicated to sustainability include the U.S. Green Building Council; the WCHBA Built Green Committee; the Energy & Environmental Building Association; the MAHB Green Built Michigan's technical advisory and remodeling advisory committees; and the NARI Remodel Green Midwest conference. With many of these organizations, Michael has been collaboratively working to develop guidelines and criteria for the implementation and evaluation of sustainable residential design.

The work of Architectural Resource has received numerous honors over the years. Recent accolades include five gold awards in the Professional Remodeler's Best of the Best Design Awards, three first-place awards from the American Institute of Building Design, four first-place accolades in the Chrysalis Design Awards and two gold awards, two Janus awards and a Best-in-Show award in Qualified Remodeler's Master Design Awards ... all in the same year. Committed firmly to the belief that great architecture comes in all shapes and sizes, one of the firm's most award-winning designs took the form of a simple, elegant 3-foot by 5-foot entryway roof addition to a Tudor residence. Architectural Resource recognizes that without the close collaboration and outstanding contributions of its builder colleagues, artisans and craftspeople that the firm's work would amount to little more than lines on paper. The firm keenly understands that it is by working closely and cooperatively with all involved parties that both great process and great product are achieved for its clients.

Going forward, Architectural Resource looks to take Green design to an even more aesthetically sophisticated level. Michael feels that the emergence of modern architecture's focus on and development of sustainable architecture—no longer solely with an emphasis on aesthetics, but performance and environmental stewardship as well—is the most exciting architectural revolution since the brick. "For all of recorded history, humanity's buildings have been accepted as essentially transgressions on the natural environment; that is changing now," Michael says. The exceptional work of Architectural Resource will certainly continue to provide clients with inspiring platforms from which to live their lives and seek to better coexist with the world we all inhabit.

Architectural Resource's maxim rings true: Imagine Inspired Design®.

RIGHT:
This Tudor residence's entryway roof addition integrates the existing home's architectural period styling. Built by Washtenaw Woodwrights.
Photograph by Stanley Livingston

FACING PAGE TOP:
This contemporary kitchen remodel and addition features a custom island and glass-tile backsplash. Built by Custom Design Build. Kitchen design by Designer Ink.
Photograph by Stanley Livingston

FACING PAGE BOTTOM:
This Craftsman-style lakeside residence was inspired by the "not-so-big" house philosophy and incorporates Green design and building. Built by W. Pennings and Sons.
Photograph by Stanley Livingston

RICHARD KLIGMAN

Superb Custom Homes

A third-generation homebuilder, Richard Kligman has been around the building industry his entire life, having learned the craft from his father, who learned from his father before him. Rich is well equipped to lead the family business into a new era, by upholding the strong tradition of service and quality established before him and by providing today's generation of custom homebuyers with an unmatched level of design and luxury.

Rich's father, Al, founded Superb Homes in 1962, and has been crafting luxurious homes in southeastern Michigan for more than four decades. Superb Homes is recognized throughout the region for exceptional quality, immaculate style and lasting value. Its most recent efforts include luxury lakefront and lake access estate homes in Northville's Stonewater at Parkshore Lake. These new homes offer the best of today's designs, luxurious appointments, quality and workmanship.

ABOVE:
The use of expansive windows, soaring ceilings, ipe flooring and earth-tone accents helps blur the line between elements of nature and design.
Photograph by Beth Singer

FACING PAGE:
Gas lanterns, sculpted limestone and impeccably designed landscaping highlight the elegant exterior of this lakefront home, which boasts approximately 8,000 square feet of finished living space.
Photograph by Beth Singer

From a young age, Rich spent considerable time on jobsites, and continued to be around homebuilding throughout his high school and college years. He joined the family business full-time after graduating from Michigan State's Building Construction Management program in 1992, becoming president of Superb Homes in 2000. In addition to managing Superb Homes, Rich founded Superb Custom Homes in 2003 and is building first-rate, estate-sized, custom residences in the Asbury Park and Normandy Hills communities in Novi, Michigan. Superb Custom Homes also designs and builds custom luxury homes for families throughout southeastern Michigan. For homeowners who love their existing home and want a truly spectacular addition or remodel, Superb Custom Remodeling will meet and exceed their expectations.

Superb Custom Homes' clients have the option of choosing from a wide array of custom home designs and exterior elevations. Then, working with a pair of interior designers, they carefully craft luxurious interiors that fit their families' lifestyles. If a client wishes to create a truly one-of-a-kind home from beginning to end, a licensed architect will meet with and help them through the process, establishing goals, concepts and lifestyle priorities that

TOP LEFT:
Combining function with form, this spacious kitchen allows for world-class cooking and is a welcome place for friends and family to gather.
Photograph by Beth Singer

BOTTOM LEFT:
After a busy day, this warm and intimate room invites the homeowner to unwind with a drink and a favorite book.
Photograph by Beth Singer

FACING PAGE TOP:
Ten-foot ceilings, abundant windows, luxurious mouldings and a gorgeous custom stone mantel create a perfect place to enjoy life and entertain.
Photograph by Beth Singer

FACING PAGE BOTTOM:
This visual work of art was derived from the client's goal to have a dramatic living room combining Mediterranean and traditional elements.
Photograph by Beth Singer

lead to an initial sketch. From there the design process continues to carefully match the homeowner's desired style and custom features. As always the unmatched quality of workmanship and service buyers receive are standards when purchasing a home by Superb Custom Homes.

Rich is committed to giving back to his local community. Each year Superb Custom Homes introduces the homebuilding craft to Michigan youth by hosting a local middle school at one of its jobsites. Students meet the craftsmen and subcontractors and learn about career opportunities. Rich is also vice president on the Building Industry Association of Southeast Michigan's executive board, serves on the state board of directors for the Michigan Association of Homebuilders, and serves on the National Board of Directors for the National Association of Homebuilders. As well, Rich is a member of Green Built™ Michigan.

Rich continues to lead the family business, and was named the 2005 Young Builder of the Year for southeastern Michigan by *Building Business & Apartment Management Magazine*. With Rich advancing the company's focus on custom homebuilding, establishing new, lasting relationships with clients and diversifying its depth and breadth of endeavors, the future of the company surely rests in superb hands.

Jonathan Lee

Jonathan Lee Architects

The son of a builder, Jonathan Lee, AIA, recalls firing brick with his father as a youngster growing up in Africa and being around building from his earliest beginnings. From historic sites in Africa and Europe to a memorable first visit to Chicago as a teen, he was exposed to exceptional architecture from a young age and his affinity for great design was cemented. In the many years since, Jonathan has traveled the globe extensively and is consistently exploring new spaces, refining his wealth of knowledge and seeking out brilliant design that informs his work.

Jonathan has long been committed to traditional design and the classical language of architecture, an approach he values for its enduring beauty, sincerity and trueness to materials. He obtained his bachelor's and master's degrees from the University of Michigan, spending his final semester of study at the Technical University of Vienna in Austria, where he worked in the studio of renowned architect Helmut Wimmer. Upon

his return stateside, Jonathan worked under Charles Warren and John Blatteau, both of whom were great influences, instilling in him historical precedent that was invaluable in influencing a young architect beyond his academic endeavors. The ability to spend long hours poring over Blatteau's impeccable library was a cherished opportunity.

In 1995 Jonathan spent a year teaching design in Italy as part of the University of Notre Dame Rome Studies Program, during which he visited 50 Italian cities, frequenting extraordinary libraries and unique destinations typically undiscovered by pedestrian tourists. He has also taught design at the Parsons School of Design and the Institute of Classical Architecture, both in New York. Jonathan founded his firm in 1999, and has since crafted exquisite traditional residences not only in Michigan, but often in New York, Florida and Massachusetts, among other locales.

ABOVE LEFT:
The hall archway mirrors in the entry arch from the vestibule, while light suffuses the corridor through triple-hung windows offering views to the porches.
Photograph by Dietrich Floeter

ABOVE RIGHT:
Opposing vanities create symmetry in this elegant master bath suite adorned with rich marble and wainscoting.
Photograph by Dietrich Floeter

FACING PAGE:
The dining room opens out to the courtyard on the lakeside terrace façade, while the screened-in tea pavilion ends the axis from the dining room to create a private courtyard with library porch beyond.
Photograph by Dietrich Floeter

Whether building the simplest of structures, such as a barn, or a complex commercial building, Jonathan holds that the orders and proportions are of the utmost importance and both are essential to enduring traditional architecture. How a building ages is also a pertinent consideration in his designs, and when appropriate materials are selected and the traditional vernacular is skillfully employed, buildings have a sophistication and lucid language that eschews association with a particular epoch—because they are built in the modern day.

Jonathan takes great pride in the handcrafted aspect of traditional design and he notes that all people have an innate ability to create beautiful things. In his never-ending quest to ultimately define what beauty is, Jonathan has traveled as much as possible, exploring shapes and spaces around the world to better inform his architectural perspective. The results of his earnest commitment to traditional design and ongoing efforts to study and understand classical languages and proportions are evidenced in each of Jonathan Lee Architects' timeless architectural solutions.

GLENDA L. MEADS
KAREN P. SWANSON
ROBERT S. SWANSON

Swanson Meads Architecture

ABOVE:
The one-story, curved cedar siding element comprises an office-study with a continuous ribbon of windows.
Photograph by Robert Saarinen Swanson

FACING PAGE:
The wedge-shaped elements of the house are solid-brick blocks, which read against the skyline. The windows frames are dark ash and a lower, projecting portico defines the entry.
Photograph by Robert Saarinen Swanson

When Glenda Meads, AIA, and Karen Swanson, AIA, first met each other as fellow adjunct design professors at the University of Detroit's Mercy School of Architecture, it was more than a standard faculty meeting—it was a truly serendipitous encounter. Sharing academic backgrounds from strong design schools—Glenda received degrees in architecture and environmental studies from the University of Waterloo while Karen got her Bachelor of Fine Arts from the University of Michigan and her Master of Architecture from the University of Illinios at Chicago—and having both recently started their own architectural practices, the collaboration was an ideal fit, and Swanson Meads Architecture was born in 1999. A small firm that seeks out projects with intrinsic individuality as the design genesis, Swanson Meads crafts architectural solutions in which innovative forms are client-tailored and derived from an essential integration with the site.

The work of Swanson Meads can be found throughout Oakland County, as well as to the north in the Traverse City, Petoskey and Harbor Springs areas and occasionally out of state, in such settings as Missouri, Montana, Connecticut and Ontario. Whether residential or commercial, traditional or contemporary, the firm strives to undertake projects with an exceptional characteristic as the design's starting point. Often times, the site is the source of this innate singularity; still others, the client's personality or program provides it.

A recently completed residence in Birmingham afforded the design team a challenging, exceptional site as well as a client enthusiastic about letting the design process runs its natural course. The result: a light-filled, modern residence thoughtfully set on a heavily wooded ravine lot sloping sharply down to a river. The home's modestly scaled front courtyard presents a subdued, one-story façade that is respective of neighbors' needs for light and views, yet as the site slopes down the ravine the residence follows the descent, giving way to a more prominent two-story composition in the back. The firm holds that varying styles can exist harmoniously among adjacent structures so long as the scale is respected and one does not overpower the other.

Another recently completed project designed for an art collector in an eclectic neighborhood in Huntington Woods produced a modern home inspired by Alvar Aalto's Carré house in France. Positioned on an elevated corner lot overlooking a small triangular park to the west, wedge-shaped forms work their way around the corner of the site and low, covered horizontal walkways tie them together.

An exciting upcoming project for Swanson Meads is an addition to the cultural center in Fenton, Michigan, which was originally designed by Eliel and Eero Saarinen, Karen's great-grandfather and great-uncle, respectively. Glenda and Karen are joined in the office by Karen's father, Robert Saarinen Swanson, AIA, who brings more than 50 years of experience to the firm.

Content to stay a boutique firm, Swanson Meads Architecture looks to continue to undertake a select number of exceptional projects, both residential and commercial, in which architectural solutions take innovative forms that are adroitly tailored to both client and site.

ABOVE:
With floor-to-ceiling views into the ravine tree tops, this living room shows a hint of the rust-red metal siding elements that punctuate the exterior and interior of the house.
Photograph by Robert Saarinen Swanson

FACING PAGE TOP:
The kitchen, which looks onto the dining and living areas beyond and opens onto a rear deck, is both elegant and functional.
Photograph by Robert Saarinen Swanson

FACING PAGE BOTTOM LEFT:
Looking from the living room and kitchen, the deck exhibits the remarkable juxtaposition of natural concrete block and rust-colored metal siding.
Photograph by Robert Saarinen Swanson

FACING PAGE BOTTOM RIGHT:
This rear elevation as viewed from the ravine showcases the living room cantilever clad in rust-red metal siding and floor-to-ceiling windows.
Photograph by Robert Saarinen Swanson

ROB MOSSBURG

The Cottage Company of Harbor Springs

Under the leadership of Rob Mossburg, The Cottage Company of Harbor Springs has built an outstanding reputation for the meticulous construction of luxurious single-family residences, traditional neighborhoods and classic, downtown live-work buildings. The firm has also attracted national attention for its focus on sensitive development and for its coveted interior design engagements. But it may be a reputation for extraordinary customer service that most clearly distinguishes The Cottage Company, the Little Traverse Association of Home Builders' 2006 "Homebuilder of the Year," from its peers.

As a third-generation builder and admitted perfectionist, Rob has been around high-quality buildings and detailed architecture for much of his life. But unlike most in his field, he brings a unique and invaluable background from the hospitality business that cemented his proclivity for providing superior customer service. Rob spent much of his early career as a consultant in both the real estate and lodging industries before co-founding a pair of hotel companies, which he sold prior to starting The Cottage Company in 2000. In his

ABOVE LEFT:
Named the Best Cluster Community in America by *Builder Magazine*, the firm's Bay Street Cottages have received national acclaim for the use of New Urbanist, smart growth and sustainable building principles. Built on a sensible scale, the freestanding cottages possess the same luxury features and quality detailing and construction as other custom homes the company builds.
Photograph courtesy of The Cottage Company of Harbor Springs

ABOVE RIGHT:
The company's headquarters in downtown Harbor Springs was named one of the best live-work buildings in the country by *Builder Magazine*. The building contains a 3,000-square-foot residence above The Cottage Company offices with an extraordinary rooftop deck overlooking Little Traverse Bay.
Photograph courtesy of The Cottage Company of Harbor Springs

previous endeavors, providing premier customer service was always of paramount importance, as J.D. Powers and Associates named his hotel company as one of the top service providers in the world. Today, The Cottage Company defines itself as being a service provider as much as a home builder and its passion for genuine customer service is simply unmatched.

Building for discriminating clients in and around Harbor Springs—an area often referred to as a "more approachable Martha's Vineyard"—The Cottage Company has become well known for building sophisticated and engaging structures in a northern Michigan cottage vernacular. Elegant yet comfortable, the style is manifested through the grand cottages it constructs and is characterized by the use of natural materials in a turn-of-the-century, often Shingle-style, design. The firm's latest project is the Hotel Janelle, an ultra-luxury boutique condominium hotel located along the waterfront in downtown Harbor Springs.

ABOVE LEFT:
This bath interior was inspired by turn-of-the-century designs and features octagonal tiles, a claw foot soaking tub and custom cabinetry designed by Rob Mossburg.
Photograph courtesy of The Cottage Company of Harbor Springs

ABOVE RIGHT:
This elegant master bedroom includes hand-carved furniture, custom art by local artists, a beadboard mantel from Cottage Company craftsmen and a custom lavender paint mix inspired by the handmade fireplace tiles.
Photograph courtesy of The Cottage Company of Harbor Springs

Outside of its daily businesses, The Cottage Company promotes ideals important to maintaining the region's high quality of life. Rob serves on the board of the Michigan Land Use Institute, whose mission is to promote smart growth in northern Michigan. As an example of walking the talk, the firm's Bay Street Cottages project, which includes 18 custom-built homes on a 1.25-acre lot, has received national acclaim for its sensible scale and detailed design that harkens back to the walkable, village neighborhoods of the late 19th century. The firm also champions sustainable building practices and efforts to combat sprawl. Rob serves on the board of the local land conservancy and he and his family have donated land for multiple conservation easements. Such donations have included permanently protecting more than a quarter-mile of scenic road frontage and using the proceeds from a development project to preserve a Centennial Farm, which was squarely in the path of suburban development. In addition, the company supports myriad local charities and has won numerous awards for outstanding citizenry.

Well known by northern Michigan residents and vacationers alike, The Cottage Company has established a phenomenal reputation for buildings of exceptional quality and is committed to smart-growth, sustainable building and, of course, extraordinary customer service—principles sure to guide this dynamic company into even greater future success.

LEFT:
The functional wet bar located in the great room's dining area contains a wine cooler and diswasher drawers. An expandable dining table with self-storing leaves, wood chandelier and handmade tile backsplash complete the ensemble.
Photograph courtesy of The Cottage Company of Harbor Springs

FACING PAGE:
Located above the firm's offices, the condominium serves as a showroom. The bright color palette is a hallmark of the firm's interiors and the wall color is a custom mix, Mossburg Green, which has been sold nationwide. The handmade wooden mantel was designed by Rob. Wide-plank wood floors with square nail heads and a coffered ceiling with inlaid beadboard panels exude sophistication.
Photograph courtesy of The Cottage Company of Harbor Springs

ANDRE M. POINEAU

Andre Poineau Woodworker, Inc.

Andre M. Poineau grew up on Lake Charlevoix and has cherished its ineffable grandeur his entire life. He knows intimately what lake living has to offer. His firm, Andre Poineau Woodworker, is exceptionally skilled at conveying the essence of lake life to homeowners through architecture, in which unparalleled attention to detail and extraordinary craftsmanship are hallmarks of timelessly original compositions.

Andre began his career in arts and crafts, creating furniture, cabinets, entry doors and other finely detailed objects, and continued to research artisanship in ensuing years, further augmenting his considerable knowledge and skills. Approximately 25 years ago his firm undertook its first design-build project, a family compound on Lake Charlevoix in which the owner saw Andre's design potential and allowed him freedom to take ownership of the design. The resulting family compound, which Andre largely credits with launching his firm, was a log house with 3,000 feet of frontage along Lake Charlevoix, a stream running through the center of it, a guest house and a covered bridge.

As a design-build firm, Andre Poineau Woodworker affords clients peace of mind as they know that design and construction are all handled under one roof, ensuring continuity and efficiently completed projects. It also assures that Andre is personally involved with every aspect of every project. While Andre does design work all over the country, the homes built by his firm have all been lakefront homes—primarily on Lake Charlevoix—and usually are set in the northwestern portion of the mitten.

His full-time architect, Paul King, will often collaborate with Andre on the design, but always makes the design a buildable reality. The firm's 15,000-square-foot woodworking shop is run by 10-plus artisans who are able to produce all types of custom doors, glasswork, metalwork, castings, etc.—Andre notes that the shop "can produce absolutely anything."

The homes designed by Andre Poineau Woodworker are all of their own theme, which is interpreted by Andre to establish an integral relationship between the home, the owner and the lake in northern Michigan. Each home, whether French Country, Adirondack cottage, Shingle style or other, is derived from an essential connection with the lake via expansive glass, transoms and tall ceilings, among other design elements. These original creations celebrate the space inside, outside and in between, limiting barriers between daily life and the water. The homes are also consistently built with natural materials, natural stones and woods, all of which are prevalently featured in Poineau creations.

ABOVE LEFT:
This classic summer cottage is removed just enough from the boater activity on Indian River to enjoy both lake living and tranquil solitude.
Photograph by Lesley Pritchard, Wildwood Photography

ABOVE RIGHT:
This timeless back porch always welcomes residents home to the river.
Photograph by Lesley Pritchard, Wildwood Photography

FACING PAGE:
A lifetime collection of watercraft and memorabilia are entrenched in the daily affairs of one lucky enough to call a boathouse home.
Photograph by Don Rutt

ABOVE LEFT:
Natural materials and organic design are an extension of the landscape for this north shore Lake Charlevoix home.
Photograph by Lesley Pritchard, Wildwood Photography

ABOVE RIGHT:
This outdoor kitchen with heated, glass block floor ensures that outdoor serenity and culinary endeavors can be enjoyed simultaneously—even on a chilly day.
Photograph by Lesley Pritchard, Wildwood Photography

FACING PAGE:
This north shore Lake Charlevoix home was designed to capture the ever-changing moods of southwest exposure on a large body of water.
Photograph by Lesley Pritchard, Wildwood Photography

For more than 25 years Andre Poineau Woodworker has designed and built finely crafted lakefront homes that epitomize the spirit of lake living in northern Michigan. Whether on Lake Charlevoix, Lake Michigan, Walloon Lake, Burt Lake or another body of water, the firm's homes encapsulate intimate lake interaction in homes adorned with sculptural aesthetics produced by the skilled artisans at Andre Poineau Woodworker.

MICHAEL PORIS

McIntosh Poris Associates

ABOVE:
Carefully placed clerestory windows let in natural light yet protect precious art.
Photograph by Balthazar Korab

FACING PAGE:
A contemporary take on traditional Prairie-style architecture, this house is made with a keen eye toward craft and art.
Photograph by Balthazar Korab

It takes a rare individual who, at the rise of an architectural career in California, would decide to return to his hometown with the express wish to effect a real difference in the urban rebirth of Detroit. Fortunately, in 1994, Michael Poris was influenced by his childhood friend and fellow architect Douglas McIntosh's vision to return to Birmingham to open the partnership of McIntosh Poris Associates.

Douglas McIntosh (1962-2006) received his master's degree in architecture from Yale University and before first founding the firm in New Haven, Connecticut, had been employed by the prestigious firm of Cesar Pelli & Associates for eight years. Drawn back to Detroit, he relocated his firm with an idealistic vision. Similarly, before co-founding his namesake firm with Douglas, Michael gained critical and regional experience from such prestigious firms as Cesar Pelli & Associates, Morphosis Architects, Frank O. Gehry & Associates and more. McIntosh Poris Associates' goal of transforming cities through strongly grounded ideals and dialogue originates from the experiences both assembled during their formative years.

Following the holistic philosophies of design set forth by Douglas and Michael, McIntosh Poris Associates' talented staff, including five architects and two interior designers, addresses around 30 projects a year. Designing for such diverse projects as single- and multiple-family residences, non-profit organizations and commercial buildings—both ground-up and rehabilitative work—Michael and his staff view their projects as a collaboration with their clients, rather than an imposition of their singular views. They believe interaction helps give rise to new relationships and meanings at multiple scales, which ultimately leads to more engaging buildings, communities and urban centers. The firm's designers have been fortunate enough to be commissioned for projects that further their love of the craft. As a direct result, they and other architects like them are witnessing a positive and refreshing architectural transformation in Detroit.

As Detroit embraces a more urban movement, Michael's education, exposure and knowledge have led him to design in the contemporary vernacular. Michael's designs reflect the present: today's lifestyles, today's varied definitions of "family" and today's needs and desires. But in defining contemporary, one must acknowledge that it is a method of designing specific residences with relevance to site and stylistic preferences, not necessarily a one-style-fits-all genre. For instance, the firm does quite a bit of appropriate historic renovation both commercially and residentially: Reborn are the row houses of years past and saved are the buildings that might have otherwise been torn down, but now have found timely, contemporary value.

The firm's work has received eight American Institute of Architects Honor Awards, 25 *Detroit Home* awards, a Masonry Institute of Michigan award, a National Trust for Historic Preservation award, a Michigan Historic Network Preservation award, a Michigan Governor's Art award and has been widely published locally, nationally and internationally.

Most important to Michael, however, is that he remains inspired by the vision of his lifelong friend, Douglas McIntosh, and that the works of McIntosh Poris Associates serve as a lasting tribute to his memory.

ABOVE LEFT:
The historic Melchers-McIntosh residence was lovingly restored.
Photograph by Kevin Bauman

ABOVE RIGHT:
The architects referred to historical photographs to create authentic interiors.
Photograph by Justin Maconcohie

FACING PAGE LEFT:
The feeling of a New York loft has been evoked in this new, light-filled contemporary home.
Photograph by Balthazar Korab

FACING PAGE RIGHT:
A double-height space with vast window walls accents the open floorplan and easy flow of space.
Photograph by Balthazar Korab

MARC RUETER

Rueter Associates Architects

Growing up in western Nebraska, Marc Rueter, AIA, was always building things, learning construction techniques from his father, a farmer, who happened to be an exceptional drawer. Marc fondly recalls sitting on his father's desk watching him sketch, and largely credits him with teaching him how to draw. From architect to city planner back to architect, Marc's circuitous road to establishing his own firm instilled in him great appreciation for historic architecture's classical organization, which Rueter Associates Architects deftly melds with a modern appreciation for light and space in a way that creates contextually appropriate, enduring architectural solutions.

Marc earned his bachelor's degree from the University of Nebraska's architecture school, a curriculum chiefly focused on modernist architecture. This was followed by the decision to study urban planning.

ABOVE LEFT:
Designed to exhibit the clients' glass and painting collections, the interiors have generous space for entertaining.
Photograph by Marc Rueter

ABOVE RIGHT:
The second-floor stair hall is separated from the study with French doors and a laminated glass transom set into drywall reglets.
Photograph by Marc Rueter

After a master's degree in city planning from the University of Wisconsin and a two-year stint as an assistant professor of architecture at the University of Kansas, Marc was employed as a planner for the city of Ann Arbor. During this five-year period Marc studied neighborhoods extensively, wrote downtown and neighborhood plans, photographed many vernacular buildings and gained an invaluable appreciation for and knowledge of classical proportions and details. However, after being away from architecture for a while he began to miss it and returned to his first passion.

Much of Rueter Associates' residential endeavors consist of historic renovations, an area of work that

was initially derived largely from the relationships forged during Marc's city-planning experience in

Ann Arbor. Such projects, or, more generally, renovations of homes designed in a historic idiom, allow

the firm to infuse interior spaces with light and incorporate modern detailing with contemporary

materials. Of course, this is skillfully achieved while maintaining the classic exteriors and preserving

the traditional shapes, volumes and proportions within.

ABOVE LEFT:
Above a busy urban street this quiet contemporary living space was inspired by Alden B. Dow's architecture.
Photograph by Geoff Harker

ABOVE RIGHT:
Complementing the skylights, low-voltage display lighting was tucked into long, recessed ceiling troughs.
Photograph by Geoff Harker

Since the mid-1980s, Rueter Associates Architects has designed an array of commercial and residential buildings, work that includes single- and multi-family housing, new construction, additions, historic preservation and renovations. Commercial projects tend to be in a more contemporary language, which offers a nice counterpoint to the largely historic residential work. An exceptional, recently completed project in Ann Arbor allowed the firm to transform a historic downtown building into a one-of-a-kind mixed-use structure with five apartments, office infill and an extraordinary penthouse perched atop the fourth story. The penthouse was characterized by fairly simple organization, forms and massing yet adorned with inconspicuous lighting fixtures and reveals as modest yet elegant details.

Collaboratively engaging in a handful of exceptional projects each year, the firm has recently become involved with designing architectural products—for example, bicycle shelters, pavilions and table-and-chair arrangements—which are customized for their particular setting and woven into the larger architecture. Carefully combining a genuine appreciation for architectural precedent and classical organization with modern sensibilities for space and light, the work of Rueter Architects Associates is timeless, engaging and respective of its surroundings.

ABOVE LEFT:
A luminous glass curtainwall wraps around the kitchen, silhouetting the iridescent, glazed glass tiles and absolute black granite counters.
Photograph by Geoff Harker

BOTTOM LEFT:
The elevator alcove and doors are faux-painted in a dark-red hammered metallic finish. The glass-topped upper display shelves are uplighted with halogen.
Photograph by Geoff Harker

FACING PAGE:
The penthouse residence sits above this mixed-use structure designed by the architect as urban infill complementing the historic building next door.
Photograph by Marcy Giannunzio

SALLY RUSSELL

Sally Russell Building Company

As the daughter of a civil engineer, Sally Russell learned how to read blueprints at an early age. Her father's drawings illustrated how large and small structural components must be considered early in the design phase to have a finished product that is both soundly engineered and structurally functional. Since founding Sally Russell Building Company in 1993, Sally has taken this early lesson into architects' offices during the design phase and then onto jobsites, where often the real challenge of harmoniously melding form and function takes place. Brokering a dialogue and finding consensus between the client, the architect and the people who make the design a reality is one of the biggest challenges for a builder, but when done successfully, results in aesthetically pleasing, functional structures. The hallmark of Sally's work is maintaining that dialogue and collaboration from beginning to end. The Sally Russell Building Company has left its unique stamp on southeast Michigan via an array of projects that unites engaging architectural forms, custom millwork and rich craftsmanship with energy-efficient, functionally sound structures.

Sally's first projects consisted of renovating her own homes. The most ambitious was a three-story farmhouse in Birmingham that spanned 17 years. These projects introduced her to some of the area's finest skilled trade subcontractors, carpenters and specialized vendors. Moreover, upon discovering such a meager selection of ready-made mouldings at local lumber companies, she purchased a Williams & Hussey molder/planer in 1978. This first piece of machinery allowed her to design, make and incorporate unique interior trims for her homes and became the impetus for assembling a variety of millwork machinery, which has been housed in the company's impressive shop since 2000. Exceptional custom millwork is a prevalent feature in many of Sally's projects and another hallmark of her work.

The experience of having her residence double as the construction site emphasized the importance of creating and adhering to efficient work schedules. Clients who choose to work with Sally Russell Building Company receive the benefit of her communication and scheduling skills in the form of projects that are completed on time and within budget.

LEFT:
The timber trusses, leaded glass windows and hand-hewn parquet floors are showcased in this 35-foot-tall great room.
Photograph by Hillary Fox

FACING PAGE LEFT:
This view of the front door is highlighted by the sweeping staircase and the mosaic, tone-on-tone oval marble floor.
Photograph by Hillary Fox

FACING PAGE RIGHT:
The award-winning china pantry features lightly glazed cabinetry and a white onyx countertop.
Photograph by Hillary Fox

The firm's portfolio is quite diverse and reflects a wide range of styles and sizes that encompasses large and small renovations, additions and new construction in both residential and commercial arenas. The differing needs and processes required of such a varied portfolio necessitate a deft ability to adapt and manage each project's specific requirements. For example, an addition of several thousand square feet to an existing manufacturing plant in Royal Oak had to unfold carefully and cleanly around the daily work routines of the firm's 80 employees. The project grew to include the remodeling of many existing rooms and offices, so the scheduling of materials and crews changed almost daily.

One of the firm's most recently completed residences was a palatial home located on Vaughan Road in Bloomfield Hills. This extraordinary, richly detailed home achieved a classic look, appearing as if it had always been there with its use of artisan-quality craftsmanship and yet included every modern-day amenity. Indubitably an exquisite haven, it has already received nine awards from *Detroit Home* magazine and one from the National Kitchen and Bath Association.

Sally is a proponent of energy conservation and believes the building industry must utilize both materials and technology to mitigate energy costs for homeowners and promote efficient use of natural resources. Each project is scanned with infrared technology after insulation is installed and before drywall is hung to ensure warm or cold air is not being lost. She is also a huge proponent of radiant heat, as it is more efficient and effective than traditional forced-air systems, which rely upon on-off cycling thermostats.

Delicately commingling resplendent forms with energy efficient, carefully crafted functionality, the award-winning work of Sally Russell Building Company—whether large, small, commercial or residential—is defined by quality craftsmanship, effective project management and a growing list of satisfied clientele.

ABOVE:
Examples of rich craftsmanship abound at every corner at the Vaughan Road home, such as this impeccable, hand-carved element from the library's fireplace surround.
Photograph by Hillary Fox

RIGHT:
The door and wrought-iron gates to the wine cellar were salvaged from a 1917 house that originally sat on the Vaughan Road property.
Photograph by Hillary Fox

FACING PAGE TOP:
The quarter-sawn, white oak library features hand-carved elements on the mantel, a wet bar and a walnut-and-oak herringbone floor.
Photograph by Hillary Fox

FACING PAGE BOTTOM:
This elegant kitchen is warmed by abundant wood and its open layout exhibits the large island, nearby breakfast cabinet and the gas cooktop alcove.
Photograph by Hillary Fox

VICTOR SAROKI

Victor Saroki & Associates Architects PC

For Victor Saroki, FAIA, designing a home constitutes more than just delicately balancing each client's personal agenda with a particular site's unique surroundings—it represents an obligation to the community in which that structure is constructed. Victor realizes that his buildings—both public and private—will long outlive him and his clients and that he has a responsibility to enhance their larger localities. His firm, Victor Saroki & Associates Architects, the 2007 AIA Michigan Firm of the Year, has been dedicated to improving the built environment in southeastern Michigan for the past quarter century, marrying harmonious design, client-tailored aesthetics and distinct site characteristics in each project it undertakes.

Victor's penchant for design was first piqued during adolescence when his father engaged in the homebuilding process. Victor sat in on meetings in which his father and the architect would review plans

ABOVE:
This conservatory is used as a family sitting room. Handcrafted and fabricated in Belgium, the room's operable lower- and upper-roof windows provide natural venting.
Photograph by Beth Singer

FACING PAGE:
Clean lines, rich materials and an impossibly blue sky define the view of this carriage house with guest quarters off the motor court.
Photograph by Beth Singer

and drawings, and not only did he understand early on how floorplans and elevations worked, but he was captivated to witness how drawings became reality. With his affinity for architecture established from that first fortuitous exposure to the craft, Victor proceeded to Lawrence Technological University to refine his technical savvy, obtaining his Bachelor of Science in architecture in 1979 and his Bachelor of Architecture in 1980. Victor started his eponymous firm in 1982 with his wife, Michelle. During his academic pursuits, Victor became friends with classmates Randal Secondino, AIA, and Mark Farlow, who have now been with the firm for more than 15 years and serve as principals.

The firm's residential work is defined by its design and quality, and each home is a unique architectural solution that responds to the client's particular lifestyle and ambitions, as well as site characteristics involving natural features, context and patterns, which include the direction that cars travel, how streets are oriented, where the sun rises and sets, and other pertinent aspects of the setting. The firm earnestly listens to its clients and will work to achieve their goals, which are often grandiose in nature. Past homes built have included features such as an indoor gymnasium that doubles as an elegant ballroom—basketball courts disappear, a chandelier comes down from the ceiling and carpet covers the gym floor—and conservatories, which involved traveling to Belgium with the client to research details regarding conservatory fabrication.

Victor was named AIA Detroit's Young Architect of the Year in 1994 and was elevated to AIA's College of Fellows in 2000. Victor Saroki & Associates Architects has won more than 50 design awards over the years, and is earnestly committed to improving Michigan's built environment via illustrious design. Victor sums up the collaborative experience frankly and succinctly: "If you put a priority on design and a priority on service, we're going to be an outstanding value."

ANTONINO SCAVO

Antonino Scavo & Associates, Inc.

ABOVE:
Emphasizing the volume through open arches, the spaces overflow into each other in this two-story living area, which is warmed by an abundance of natural materials.
Photograph by Michael Raffin

FACING PAGE:
This updated Tudor-style residence on a breathtaking lake lot was challenging because of its owner's exacting attention to detail from exterior to interior.
Photograph by Michael Raffin

The son of a mason, Antonino Scavo grew up around the construction industry his entire life in southeast Michigan, gaining valuable exposure to subdivisions and new construction in the residential market from an early age. When he won several drafting awards in statewide high school competitions sponsored by *The Detroit News*—which in many ways first elucidated his proclivity for cunning design—it became obvious that his affinity for architecture was more than just a passing predilection, but rather an innate talent that needed to be honed and explored.

Seeking to refine that inherent skill, Antonino completed the architecture curriculum at the highly regarded Lawrence Technological Institute in Southfield. After graduation, Antonino worked at a small firm in Clinton Township as a draftsman, working his way up to office manager and establishing valuable relationships with developers, builders and subcontractors that are still paying dividends today. After 14 years, Antonino

left to start his own eponymous firm, and has been designing and building sophisticated structures comprising much of southeast Michigan's built environment in that role for more than a decade.

A small firm consisting of four designers, Antonino and his secretary, Antonino Scavo & Associates prides itself on making every home it designs a new and fresh experience. Antonino ensures that each residence is tailored to the individual, and it is the smile on his clients' faces when they see their built-out dream home—the translation from the initial meetings' conceptual contemplations into a finished, tangible reality—that he finds genuinely rewarding.

No matter how whimsical or extravagant a request may be, clients rest assured that Antonino will work diligently to realize their ambitions. Unique elements previously incorporated into clients' homes include a refrigerated, humidified wine room with multiple components, saunas able to accommodate 10 to 12 people and an indoor swimming pool in a home that has a spiral staircase and a slide wrapping around a nook balcony down into the pool. Built on a steep but captivating lot with challenging site grades, the pool is actually housed in the basement and fully enclosed, but has three sides open to the outside thanks to a profusion of glass.

Antonino also dabbles in building, and often builds a couple of homes per year, which has helped him to better comprehend some of the difficulties associated with translating drawings to physical construction and then implementing the necessary modifications along the way. Antonino Scavo & Associates also undertakes multiple commercial projects each year, ranging from restaurants and office buildings to commercial complexes and a vibrant new water park in Kimball Township.

Going forward, Antonino expects his namesake firm to continue to grow, hopefully add a few new offices and expand into additional areas of the state. But for this mason's son with a deft hand and aptitude for design, no matter how much Antonino Scavo & Associates grows in the future, the end goal steadfastly remains to help clients envision and attain their dreams.

RIGHT:
The high-gloss marble foyer with its free-form oval stairway and overlook invites one to peer in and experience the engaging elegance.
Photograph by Michael Raffin

FACING PAGE:
The kitchen was kept intimate with soft-toned cabinet finishes and elegant lighting yet remains any cook's dream thanks to state-of-the-art appliances and functionality.
Photograph by Michael Raffin

THOMAS SEBOLD & ASSOCIATES, INC.

Thomas Sebold & Associates' client list includes some of the Great Lakes State's most prominent business owners and professionals. Respected interior designers, architects, celebrities and other well-known residents live in Sebold-built homes. From Oakland County's contemporary masterpieces and elegant traditional estates to waterfront retreats along Lake Michigan, the company's influence is far-reaching and felt throughout the state.

Collectively, the TSA team builds approximately 20 high-end homes per year ranging in size from 5,000 to 35,000 square feet. While custom estates are TSA's specialty, office buildings, retail centers, country clubs and high-end condominium developments are other projects that have been added to the team's successful history.

ABOVE:
With simple, elegant interiors and expansive windows, this 18th-century-style home, replicating those located along the James River in Virginia, is a modernized and contemporary Michigan classic. Interior design by Ingles & Associates.
Photograph by Balthazar Korab

FACING PAGE:
This Bloomfield Township estate emphasizes neoclassical design characteristics with repeated use of proportion and grace. The use of large but simple geometric shapes reflects this new-age classical design. Architecture by Hugh Newell Jacobson. Landscape architecture by Grissim Metz Andriese Associates, Inc.
Photograph by Balthazar Korab

During its half century of existence, the firm has worked with some of the most respected in the business, including Minoru Yamasaki, architect of the World Trade Center, and renowned architect Hugh Newell Jacobson, known for his fresh take on American vernacular style.

Thomas Sebold founded the Bloomfield Hills, Michigan, headquarters in 1955. An architect by trade, he gradually shifted the firm's energies from design to construction, concentrating on the luxury custom home market. Through the following decades, TSA quickly built an enviable reputation for homes crafted with the highest levels of quality and integrity.

ABOVE:
Located on a private lake, this estate contains 125 Bradford pear trees that were strategically placed and meticulously chosen to grow at the same rate, maintaining the same look and effect. Architecture by Hugh Newell Jacobson. Landscape architecture by Grissim Metz Andriese Associates, Inc.
Photograph by Balthazar Korab

FACING PAGE LEFT & RIGHT:
Handcrafted and uniquely engineered by TSA, these oversized windows combine 18th-century style with the latest window technologies. Using a counterbalance system, these double-hung windows can be easily lifted to create a transition from windows to doorways, allowing the homeowner to walk out onto the lakefront patio. Similar to this system, the library contains windows, screens and plantation shutters that slide into a hidden pocket within the library bookcase, keeping them out of view while not in use. Architecture by Hugh Newell Jacobson. Interior design by Ingles & Associates.
Photographs by Balthazar Korab

Thomas Sebold & Associates still bears its founder's name, even though Thomas' son, Dan, took over the reigns of the company in 1994. As president and principal, Dan carries on the family's legacy by personally overseeing each project to ensure that it is built to TSA's exacting specifications and expectations.

Dan's continuing leadership has given Thomas Sebold & Associates a reputation and client list that is second to none in the high-end custom residential market. His eye for detail and his vast knowledge of building materials and techniques have enabled him to set and, more importantly, to meet the highest quality standards for the company. Dan's acute awareness of alternative building materials and techniques has also enabled him to create innovative engineering solutions without compromising design intent or architectural integrity of budget-sensitive projects. His hands-on approach and involvement with each project throughout its duration is unsurpassed in the construction industry.

TOP & BOTTOM LEFT:
Intending to blend in with the landscape and appearing to grow out of the ground, this Frank Lloyd Wright-inspired estate has oversized mahogany eaves and a low-pitched Bermuda copper roof. The spacious living room features gold leaf ceilings, limestone columns and the use of numerous wood veneers. The fireplace incorporates unique materials like sapele and ebony woods in addition to bronze and stainless steel details to create a focal point. Architecture by Luckenbach | Zeigelman PLLC. Landscape architecture by Grissim Metz Andriese Associates, Inc. Interior design by Eric Charles Design.
Photographs by Balthazar Korab

FACING PAGE LEFT & RIGHT:
Use of Fond du Lac stone in the exterior design as well as the interior spaces is one of the many uses of nature throughout this Birmingham home. Horizontal bands of mahogany-framed windows are also a continuous element used in the design, allowing natural light to flood the space. Architecture by Luckenbach | Zeigelman PLLC. Interior design by Eric Charles Design.
Photographs by Balthazar Korab

Throughout the years, Dan has overseen the construction of hundreds of distinctive, high-end homes while guiding the growth of the company. TSA's talented team currently includes 30 dedicated and talented professionals. In addition to the Bloomfield Hills headquarters, a northern Michigan office was opened in 1995 to oversee the development of the 30,000-square-foot, mixed-use Bay Harbor Yacht Club. The new office represented a natural progression for the firm, and the first of a growing collection of projects in and near Petoskey. The Petoskey area remains an important part of the company's strategic goals.

In 2007, long-time employee Glenn Kunnath joined Dan as partner, vice-president and director of field operations. "Glenn has been with the company for more than 14 years and has been a major contributor to our success since joining TSA," Dan says. "He started as a project manager, moved up to vice president and is now partner. He has held every possible management position through his construction career. Glenn has proven the ability of maintaining schedules, budgets and lasting client relationships. He is an expert at delivering a project on time and on budget. Glenn is highly organized, excellent in the field and an overall credit to the company."

LEFT:
This northern Michigan home incorporates numerous large windows, capturing 180-degree views of Bay Harbor Lake and Lake Michigan beyond. A boathouse adjacent to the dock allows the homeowner to conveniently store a yacht up to 45 feet long. A window wall visually connects the living room to the boathouse, showcasing the owner's yacht. Architecture by Young & Young Architects.
Photograph by Meadows & Co. Photography

FACING PAGE LEFT & RIGHT:
This circular master bathroom located on the home's highest level features landside and waterfront views of Bay Harbor at its best. This dramatic space includes a skylight and clerestory windows to maximize natural light from sunrise to sunset. Situated to face the lake, this master bedroom represents the feeling of being at the bow of a ship. Interior design by Pace Interior Design.
Photographs by Meadows & Co. Photography

With 35 years of construction experience, Dan stands firmly behind TSA and the company's unwavering commitment to quality. Through their personal involvement in the construction process, Dan and his team build lasting relationships with their clients.

"TSA has built its reputation by insisting on the highest standards in the business. We're proud of our attention to detail and our passion for excellence," Dan says. Wherever the location, TSA's goal is to make those qualities the cornerstone of each and every home it builds.

"I am honored to continue the tradition started by my father over a half century ago," Dan says. "The majority of our business comes from referrals and former customers. We feel these referrals speak volumes about our work and honor my father's legacy. We've been involved in the construction of some amazing homes, but after 50 years we still believe that the most enduring thing we've built is our reputation."

RIGHT:
Bold colors, high-quality materials and dynamic forms, combined with endless views, make this home a summertime dream getaway. Architecture by Young & Young Architects. Landscape architecture by Vidosh Landscaping Centres.
Photograph by Meadows & Co. Photography

FACING PAGE:
Easy boathouse access makes this living room ideal for entertaining friends and family during summertime Michigan getaways. Warm colors, soft finishes and comfortable furnishings welcome guests to walk off the boat and into the living room. Architecture by Young & Young Architects. Interior design by Pace Interior Design.
Photograph by Meadows & Co. Photography

ABOVE:
This northern Michigan home situated in Bay Harbor is an exquisite example of balance and symmetry. Architectural features, landscape placement and a prominent front entry showcase the home's individuality. Architecture by Alexander V. Bogaerts + Associates. Landscape architecture by Vidosh Landscaping Centres.
Photograph by Michael Buck Studio

FACING PAGE:
Panoramic lake views offer a strong connection to the surrounding landscape with Lake Michigan to the north and Bay Harbor Lake to the south. Rich wood tones and natural materials create a warm and comforting environment for this vacation retreat. Interior design by Caryn Satovsky-Siegel.
Photographs by Michael Buck Studio

JOSH TOBIAS

Tobias Construction, Inc.

Tobias Construction is dedicated to helping its clientele attain their dreams, and an immaculate, intimately tailored residence carefully crafted by Tobias Construction is, for numerous satisfied customers, a realization that not only meets those dreams—but exceeds them beyond their wildest imagination.

Josh Tobias has long been around the building industry, engaging in a variety of landscaping jobs with his brother's company early in his career. He proceeded to complete Michigan State's construction management program in 1991, and started his own firm immediately after. Tobias Construction has built an array of stunning houses over the ensuing years, but the firm does not just build impeccable custom homes, it also offers remodeling, commercial and, of course, landscaping services. The company has worked with a number of different architects and designers over the years, many of whom have exceptionally different styles and approaches, which has made Tobias Construction a multifaceted firm that can meet any requests.

ABOVE:
The wrought-iron and wood stairway and immaculate chandelier above exude an air of sophistication in this 24-foot rotunda foyer.
Photograph by Josh Tobias

FACING PAGE:
This contemporary, 9,000-square-foot home with indoor lap pool is defined by its horizontal rooflines and ample fenestration.
Photograph by Josh Tobias

ABOVE LEFT:
This marble hallway with rounded arches and plaster, groin-vaulted ceiling exhibits rich craftsmanship and attention to detail.
Photograph by Josh Tobias

ABOVE RIGHT:
This contemporary great room-dining room combination provides the owner with extraordinary lake views.
Photograph by Josh Tobias

FACING PAGE TOP:
With its stone fireplace and barn-beam ceiling, the family room is an ideal space for leisurely respite.
Photograph by Josh Tobias

FACING PAGE BOTTOM:
The European garden terrace, featuring an Italian fountain and Mediterranean nuances, creates a tranquil outdoor setting overlooking the water.
Photograph by Josh Tobias

Working with numerous tradesmen over the years, Josh has assembled a close-knit group of craftsmen and subcontractors who work well together, look out for each other and ensure that the building process moves along quickly and without glitches. Moreover, Josh runs Tobias Construction as an open-book builder with his homeowners, guaranteeing that clients know all possible options and the cost of each. The open-book approach combined with Josh's adroit team of tradesmen provides clients with efficient, cost-effective results of the utmost quality.

In addition to undertaking light commercial projects, like building shopping centers and restaurants, Tobias Construction does a number of interior build-outs, particularly in the downtown Lansing area, much of which is undergoing a renovation. Tobias

Construction provides landscaping services with every home it builds as well, offering clients peace of mind that their builder is tackling the project from property line to property line and will be content only when the project is 100 percent complete.

Tobias Construction recently completed construction on an immaculate 10,000-square-foot home in Orchard Lake, Michigan, melding the firm's adroit building prowess with an extraordinary Lou DesRosiers design for a one-of-a-kind dream home. A grand circular driveway and all-limestone front entryway create an inviting approach for guests, before a dynamic entry foyer dazzles within. A 24-foot by 24-foot rotunda welcomes guests inside, while a sculptural-quality circular stair and an 8-foot skylight with a chandelier hanging down the middle immediately captivate. A rounded, highly detailed ceiling with exquisite paintings completes the striking ambience.

Already highly regarded for its exceptional homes, Tobias Construction looks to continue to produce first-rate work for satisfied clientele in commercial, renovation and custom homebuilding endeavors. Providing a wide range of services of utmost quality, carefully crafted by its family of superior tradesmen, the firm will surely continue to satisfy its clients beyond their expectations.

DOMINICK TRINGALI

Dominick Tringali Architects, Inc.

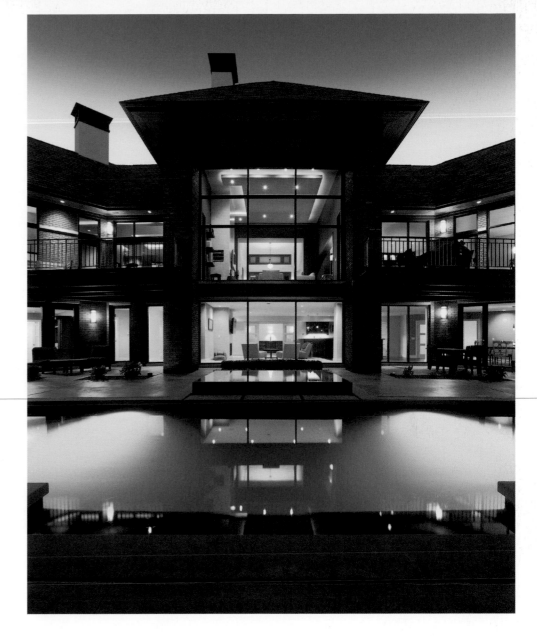

It seems Dominick Tringali was destined to be an architect—whether influenced by legacy or as the fortuitous result of his Italian-born parents' commitment to seeing that their children connect with their rich heritage. It was while visiting Italy that Dominick had the opportunity to view the larger-than-life Roman architecture firsthand. Seeing some of the greatest examples of architecture and most enduring structures ever built had a profound effect: By age 12, Dominick knew he would be an architect.

Continually encouraged by his parents and guided by their culture, Italy again beckoned Dominick, and he studied classical architecture in Florence. Upon graduation from Michigan's Lawrence Technological University in 1986, he realized the culmination of hard work and a childhood dream.

After gaining critical real-world experience and having already partnered in a successful firm in Michigan, Dominick went on to found Bloomfield Hills-based Dominick Tringali Architects in 1996, which primarily

addresses custom residential needs with a measure of select commercial projects. Built on an established philosophy of personalized design wrought by people and their lifestyles, as well as layout and the surrounding architecture and landscape, Dominick Tringali Architects is dedicated to elevating the lives of its clients by giving them the homes of their dreams while ensuring the best value for their money. Value in design is important to the firm, whether the home will be the first ever for an excited young couple, the lifelong vision of a 30,000-square-foot sanctuary realized, or the retirement residence for a seasoned couple.

These principles, combined with extensive traveling throughout the United States in order to research what makes a "great" community, formed the firm's beliefs in the social and residential benefits of New Urbanism. The firm also supports this conviction with vast knowledge on the history and foundation

of architecture and which details will balance the interior of a home. Dominick is a licensed interior designer and a member of the Institute of Classical Architecture and numerous councils, committees and programs that raise the institution of architecture's integrity. Other members of the firm hold membership in the American Institute of Architects, U.S. Green Build Council, Urban Land Institute and the Congress of New Urbanism.

Master-planned communities nurture a feeling of community and unite complementary, yet unique and interesting design. Communities like these feature homes ranging in size from under 3,000 to well over 10,000 square feet and are created to be family-friendly or expressly for senior citizens. Clients' desired square footage, coupled with their needs, presents the firm with the opportunity to flex its design muscle, offering an attention to detail and built-in amenities traditionally reserved only for luxury homes. Fueling

ABOVE:
This Country French manor has a dramatic front entry and motor court. Paul Samartino, Associate AIA, project designer.
Photograph by Beth Singer

FACING PAGE LEFT:
This home is distinctive French Eclectic in style. J.R. Ruthig, Associate AIA, project designer.
Photograph by James Haefner Photography

FACING PAGE RIGHT:
A unique outdoor living space, designed in the rear yard of this home, makes the most of a very narrow lot.
J.R. Ruthig, Associate AIA, project designer.
Photograph by James Haefner Photography

this design excellence is the belief that every house should be designed well—from conservative to expansive.

When meeting with each client, Dominick Tringali Architects addresses three factors: initial design, engineering and structure, as well as the optimal placement on the site, and how the home will eventually be detailed. Most importantly, each member of the firm does a great amount of research and is committed to being wholly interactive with and supportive of their clients' desires.

Licensed in 10 different states, this broad exposure offers another opportunity for the firm's designs to remain fresh and influenced by specific geographic preferences. While the Midwest remains more classically rooted than other parts of the country with designs ranging from Colonial Revival to French and Tudor Eclectic, those same homeowners often desire to take more design "risk" in a secondary home. From waterfront spots in Michigan, South Carolina and Florida, these vacation homes offer a wide spectrum of experimentation that has yielded exciting log homes and even a gorgeous, nautically themed residence. The secondary home market is such a large part of the firm that the architects even have plans for a satellite office in South Carolina to efficiently accommodate their clients' needs.

With a team of 25—including three licensed architects, five actively seeking their licenses and future LEED certification in the works—Dominick Tringali Architects is also continually moving toward more sustainable and efficiently built homes. Not just an idealistic vision, the firm even offers a "Healthy Home Package" while incorporating simple, yet impactful design and structural elements.

In further nurturing the flow of ideas and communication between designer and client, Dominick Tringali Architects employs the wisdom of and has forged successful relationships with some of the most influential and honored builders throughout the United States. Since its inception, the firm has been recognized yearly with multiple awards, some of which include *HOUR Detroit* magazine design awards, Parade of Homes design awards, 2006 Zweig White "Top 20 Architectural Firms to Work For," and in 2004, the firm was named among the "100 Best and Brightest Companies to Work For" by the *Detroit Free Press*.

ABOVE:
The brilliant focal point of this striking hand-carved, main stairway is the antique stained-glass window panel designed into the framework. Interior design by Dominck Tringali, AIA, NCARB.
Photograph by James Haefner Photography

RIGHT:
The main gallery hallway features French limestone floors and a handsome groin-vaulted ceiling. Interior design by Dominick Tringali, AIA, NCARB.
Photograph by James Haefner Photography

FACING PAGE:
The residence features a breathtaking integrated waterfall and front terrace. J.R. Ruthig, Associate AIA, project designer.
Photograph by Beth Singer

MICHAEL VAN GOOR

Van Goor Architects, Inc.

ABOVE:
Upon entrance, guests are met with the volume of the entire cylinder and the two-story wall of glass, while the interior space flows into the landscape.
Photograph by Howard Doughty

FACING PAGE:
The warmth of the interior space is inviting for formal evening gatherings as well as casual visits.
Photograph by Howard Doughty

The initial site visit with architect Michael Van Goor may take a bit longer than would typically be expected, but the resulting residence months later leaves no question as to the value of the time spent. His careful attention to initial details such as site orientation, circulation, views, natural features of the property and more specific personal details—ultimate goals of the family, desires, lifestyle—coalesce into a final design that undeniably says "home" to the family for whom it was created.

After finishing his bachelor's degree and receiving his master's degree at the University of Michigan College of Architecture and Urban Planning, Michael's affinity for Ann Arbor sealed his choice as to where to begin his career and is, of course, where he eventually set up his practice. Established in 1994, the full-service firm of Van Goor Architects represents excellence in design, planning and construction, and services the residential, commercial and entertainment industries.

The firm is located in a renovated historic building in downtown Ann Arbor, and its success has been built upon the demonstration of professional skills and personal commitment to clients. Ann Arbor and surrounding areas provide opportunities to work with diverse housing mediums, such as custom homes ranging from 1,600 to 10,000 square feet and multi-family projects—including loft apartments downtown. Such diversity has allowed Van Goor Architects to keep pace with current trends in the housing industry. The academic atmosphere of Ann Arbor also lends itself to the receptiveness of Green building techniques, which the firm employs as much as budgets will allow. Sustainable building practices are of particular importance to Michael, a member of the Green Building Council. He presents his clients with options that enable them to make well-informed decisions for their homes and lifestyles.

Although many firms tend to eschew rehabilitation projects, Michael enjoys the lessons they teach and finds inherent value in them. The opportunity to sympathetically meld cutting-edge materials and techniques in an older home hones and strengthens the designers' problem-solving skills and experience. Renovation work dovetails with

TOP LEFT:
The design of the fireplace and media built-in shelving translates the circular form from plan to elevation.
Photograph by Howard Doughty

BOTTOM LEFT:
The kitchen opens to the family room for informal entertaining and daily use.
Photograph by Howard Doughty

FACING PAGE LEFT:
Different geometric forms and materials distinguish the diverse intent of the functions encompassed in each volume.
Photograph by Howard Doughty

FACING PAGE RIGHT:
The living room is open to the dining room, creating flexibility for family gatherings and entertaining large groups, as well as seating up to 25 around the dining table.
Photograph by Howard Doughty

new design, allowing those working on existing homes to see what did and did not work. Knowledgeable and thoughtful site orientation in all homes is vital—whether located on a lakefront, in town or along the countryside. This is particularly true in Michigan where a varied climate requires homes to plan for a buffer from northwest winter winds, and also benefit from southwest breezes during the precious summer months. Michael finds it disconcerting that many homes seemingly are designed without consideration to the context of the site.

Although his projects have been showcased in the Parade of Homes and featured in newspaper and magazine articles, Michael is most satisfied to be living his lifelong dream by designing the homes of his clients' dreams.

WAYNE VISBEEN

Visbeen Associates, Inc.

ABOVE:
Sunset View's dovecotes, varying roof angles and compelling peaks and gables are a nod to the past.
Photograph by William J. Hebert

FACING PAGE:
Fresh-faced style characterizes this charming cottage, which combines period details such as lap siding, stone details and transom windows with a contemporary floorplan and updated amenities.
Photograph by William J. Hebert

"Drawing lives" is Visbeen Associates' specialty. In a single meeting, the firm's principal, Wayne Visbeen, AIA, IIDA, could easily go through 20 or 30 sheets of paper—he prefers to sketch while attentively listening to and casually conversing with clients, often presenting them with an initial floorplan and some exterior perspectives by the meeting's conclusion. His keen listening and artistic skills were fine-tuned many years ago while serving as the retail designer of choice for numerous high-end retail giants across the country and abroad. Wayne and his associates are widely respected by clients and peers alike for their deft ability to visualize in three dimensions and elucidate design concepts to others.

Wayne founded his namesake firm in 1992; his unique retail design background provides an invaluable foundation for his residential architecture endeavors. He has designed more than 100 stores across

the globe from Hong Kong to the Philippines, throughout Europe to Brazil—and has procured such high-profile clients as Ralph Lauren, Banana Republic and Martha Stewart, to name a few. Another avenue for Wayne's accomplished retail design has been museum shops, which he has designed for the Louvre in Paris and the New York Metropolitan Museum of Art, among others.

His experience in retail design has greatly influenced his architectural work, introducing him to a medley of disparate styles and fine-tuning his appreciation for consistency and function within each. A key tenet of Visbeen Associates' design process is to make interior design decisions in concert with the rest of the architecture for a cohesive and functional result. Again, using lessons taken from his retail design exposure, Wayne strives to make nearly every view from within a home one of beauty, symmetry and impact.

TOP RIGHT:
This exceptional home, which won a Best in American Living award for best one-of-a kind custom home, interprets vintage 1920s' Shingle style in a contemporary but amiable rendition.
Photograph by William J. Hebert

BOTTOM RIGHT:
This enduring European-inspired design, recipient of an award of excellence for best custom home by the American Institute of Building Design, features a centralized brick courtyard with a fountain, exterior stucco and stone and a classic clay tile roof.
Photograph by Chuck Heiney

FACING PAGE LEFT:
Winner of a Best in American Living award for best one-of-a-kind custom home, Pemberley has a timeless, elegant exterior and each living space—indoors and out—is packed with unpretentious, family-friendly living. The picturesque roofline stretches and angles, enlivened by varying peaks, eaves, gables, chimneys and textures. This Old World-inspired residence appears to emerge from its natural surroundings, emitting a sense of history, warmth and authenticity.
Photograph by Michael Buck

FACING PAGE RIGHT:
Inspired by historic homes in America's grand old neighborhoods, this home combines the rich character and architectural craftsmanship of the past with contemporary conveniences. Touches of the ever-popular Shingle style—from the cedar lap siding to the pitched roof—imbue the home with all-American charm.
Photograph by Michael Buck

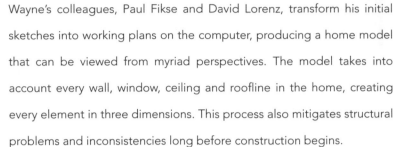

Wayne's colleagues, Paul Fikse and David Lorenz, transform his initial sketches into working plans on the computer, producing a home model that can be viewed from myriad perspectives. The model takes into account every wall, window, ceiling and roofline in the home, creating every element in three dimensions. This process also mitigates structural problems and inconsistencies long before construction begins.

At this stage, David paints a watercolor rendering of the proposed home, allowing the client to visualize and refine color choices and other cosmetic details. David's brilliant watercolor paintings so resemble their actual built-out forms that 150 of them hang framed in Visbeen Associates' office, serving as a mini-portfolio to prospective clients.

While Wayne's foray into residential architecture was initially an effort to spend more time with his family, ironically, these days his residential work is drawing him away from Grand Rapids more and more. While three-fourths of his residential endeavors still take place in Michigan, recent projects have lured him nationally and internationally to locations like

TOP LEFT:
Multiple porches, a lower-level walkout and varying roof lines exude a relaxed, easy-going elegance to these homes, which are part of a resort community of 30-plus homes on Lake Michigan designed by Visbeen Associates.
Photograph by William J. Hebert

BOTTOM LEFT:
This extraordinary home, part of the same Lake Michigan resort community, exhibits an all-American design that merges the best of the past and the needs of the present for a classic yet contemporary style.
Photograph by William J. Hebert

FACING PAGE:
Balmy breezes are felt in this coastal Southern Plantation-style cottage in the Bahamas, which blends down-home comfort with upscale style. An inviting façade and wide porch welcome friends and family.
Photograph by Visbeen Associates, Inc.

Costa Rica and the Bahamas. Not long ago, Wayne had the exciting opportunity to design his own dream home, a process he thoroughly enjoyed because, "I'm the one client who will not compromise on anything," he says. The resulting turn-of-the-century, Shingle-style home won three Best in American Living Awards from the National Association of Home Builders as the best home in the Midwest region. One of those was a gold award for best one-of-a kind custom home in the country. A recipient of numerous awards, the firm recently collected three additional Best in American Living Awards for three other Visbeen-designed homes.

Further expanding the Visbeen enterprise, Wayne has gotten involved in the project development side of the equation in order to ensure consistency within a community. For example, Wayne has designed a community known as Ravenswood, which consists of 30 Victorian-inspired cottages on White Lake. Of course, Visbeen Associates' top priority remains working passionately with clients to craft their dream homes and never compromising until a functional, aesthetically pleasing solution results.

NICHOLAS J. WHITE

N.J. White Associates

Nicholas J. White, AIA, has long been acquainted with northern Michigan's unmistakable charm—as a kid he summered among the region's lakefront cottages before working construction jobs there in high school and college, and for nearly three decades his firm has officed in Petoskey. Nick intimately knows the nuances of the northern Michigan cottage vernacular. Eschewing design gimmicks and fleeting stylistic whims, N.J. White Associates designs lasting residences that are born from a process of discovery between the client and architect, and result in timeless homes that delight owners for years to come. The completion of a project is truly anything but the end of the client-architect relationship, as Nick firmly believes that quality architecture and quality friendships endure.

After first earning a degree in fine arts from Ohio Wesleyan University, Nick found a practical application for his artistic affinities in the domain of architecture, proceeding to complete his degree in architecture from

the University of Cincinnati. Nick worked for an assortment of architecture and engineering firms in Michigan and Ohio prior to establishing his own firm in 1979. Petoskey-based N.J. White Associates is committed to supporting the local economy through the use of local materials and a skilled cadre of local craftsmen and subcontractors.

The designs of N.J. White Associates are deeply rooted in the client and are reflective of the detailed design and programming process clients engage in. This dialog between the client and the architect is a process of discovery, in which not only are the essential floorplan elements determined but individual spaces are then examined and further refined. This well-organized method ensures an efficient and smoothly run process throughout design and construction. One of the firm's more recent designs was for a resort home built on a narrow lot in the dunes fronting Lake Michigan in which the owner desired to have a home that would be comfortable for two yet capable of hosting a party for 200. The ensuing design satisfied the owner's desires via an open and flexible floorplan, an expansive lakeside porch and the implementation of a family kitchen, catering kitchen and outdoor kitchen overlooking the lake, among other design features. This home is one of the firm's many designs that has been

TOP RIGHT:
Respect for the Victorian neighborhood inspired the design of this Harbor Springs residence.
Photograph by N.J. White

BOTTOM RIGHT:
Reclaimed barnwood and rustic stone reflect the natural setting of this Lake Michigan home.
Photograph by N.J. White

FACING PAGE:
Set in a dune overlooking Lake Michigan this home settles quietly on its site.
Photograph by N.J. White

publicized, and N.J. White Associates has been featured in *Architectural Digest*, *Midwest Living*, *Detroit Monthly* and on HGTV.

In addition to Nick's support of the local economy and participation in local organizations, he has served as a team leader for annual construction missions to Cuba through the United Methodist Volunteers in Mission. Nick has made seven trips to Cuba—and has plans to return in the future—in which he and others have worked to restore old churches and parsonages that were abandoned under Communism. While the Cuban government has long been averse to such efforts, restrictions have waned over the years and enabled these commendable endeavors to continue and expand in scope.

In more recent years N.J. White Associates has had the opportunity to take commissions beyond the state of Michigan, engaging in projects in Florida, Alabama, Indiana, Nevada and other settings. Whether in Michigan or elsewhere, the firm will continue to design timeless homes that reflect the dreams and needs of its clients—who often become friends and are frequently a source of repeat design opportunities— because enduring architecture and relationships are truly hallmarks of N.J. White Associates.

ABOVE:
This quaint Victorian home graces the village in Bay Harbor near Petoskey.
Photograph by N.J. White

FACING PAGE TOP:
Hickory and fieldstone create a cozy living room in Cross Village. Interior designer D. J. Kennedy complemented
the architecture with rustic grace.
Photograph by N.J. White

FACING PAGE BOTTOM:
Perched on a Lake Michigan dune, this traditional home commands the sunset shore.
Photograph by N.J. White

ROGER WIDING

Widing Custom Homes, Inc.

ABOVE:
The double Dutch door with speakeasy, heated steps and porch, and barreled ceiling provides a charming second entrance.
Photograph by Cherry Creek Studios

FACING PAGE:
This Old World, custom-designed family estate encompasses 8,650 square feet and affords sweeping vistas of Grand Traverse Bay.
Photograph by Cherry Creek Studios

As a fourth-generation builder, Roger Widing learned from those before him that the foundation of any successful business is built on reputation, and for more than three decades he has built Widing Custom Homes into a company that prides itself on building homes of the utmost quality and attention to detail. Roger's personal philosophy is that each home he builds receives the same dedication that it would if it were his own home, and that principle has manifested itself in exquisite creations throughout northern Michigan that carry the hallmarks of Widing Custom Home's longstanding excellence.

Roger founded Widing Custom Homes in 1976 and has maintained a bona fide hands-on approach to building. In fact, his firm only builds about five homes per year—all within a roughly 60-mile radius of Traverse City—so that he is able to visit every jobsite on a daily basis. While all of the company's suppliers and subcontractors are specialists in their chosen fields and have worked with Widing Custom Homes

for years, Roger adheres to the principle that there is no substitute for personally inspecting the work on each home he builds—down to the smallest detail.

When collaborating with a client on building a one-of-a-kind dream residence, Roger brings the same devotion to the project as he does with a personal homebuilding endeavor—which he has undertaken several times. In addition to providing enjoyable opportunities to create novel features and spaces—the home that Roger is currently building will include such amenities as a 12-seat, stepped theater; a full-size gym with ample exercise equipment; a two-story, round library; and a 500-bottle wine room and adjacent tasting room, which are completely outfitted in stone from top to bottom, creating a distinctive cavern aura—the experiences have informed Roger's work, better enabling him to guide clients in their own homebuilding pursuits.

Each Widing Custom Home is unlike any other the firm has built, and exceptional requests are often a part of the process in building a one-of-a-kind home. A previously built home includes a seemingly

LEFT:
Visitors to the wine cellar and tasting room are greeted by an iron gate depicting a vineyard scene while a flagstone floor and stone, cave-like ceiling procure an earthy aura within.
Photograph by Cherry Creek Studios

FACING PAGE TOP:
The covered outdoor kitchen features granite countertops, sink, refrigerator, barbecue and grill, bringing indoor amenities to Michigan's great outdoors.
Photograph by Cherry Creek Studios

FACING PAGE BOTTOM:
Knotty alder custom cabinetry along with heated and tumbled limestone flooring, granite countertops and 12-foot ceilings make this kitchen the most popular family spot.
Photograph by Cherry Creek Studios

ordinary bookcase around a fireplace in a gentleman's library, except that when a specific place on one of the bookshelves is touched—perhaps a single book—the bookshelf opens up, uncovering a secret room. While customization is certainly a key element in each home the firm builds, rich detail and trim work are found in every home built. Roger considers exceptional round and curved trim work to be one of his firm's trademarks, and his homes are often recognized for their extraordinary detail. Challenging, round rooms and spaces are also prevalent in Widing Custom Homes, as well as elaborate mouldings—crown mouldings included in elegant dining rooms often feature upward of 16 or 18 components.

Combining a lifetime's building experience with an uncompromising devotion to unmatched quality and detail learned from his father and grandfathers before him, Roger Widing has established Widing Custom Homes as one of northern Michigan's premier custom builders, which is singularly devoted to providing clients an enjoyable building experience that culminates with the completion of the perfect home for their family.

ROBERT WINTERS
KAREN WINTERS

Winters Design Group

Growing up on the East Coast, Robert Winters, AIA, fondly recalls a host of influences that shaped his affinity for architecture. As a youth Robert passed many hours in the presence of his father's homebuilding endeavors, and these early introductions sparked his interest in "the wonderful smell of sawdust." His father, who built speculative homes on the side, worked in New York City, and the family often traveled into this international metropolis, exposing him to the iconic buildings that comprise its unmistakable architectural character. From family vacations along the Jersey Shore a great admiration was born for the various interpretations of Shingle style found in cottages dotting the Atlantic coast.

After studying architecture at Calvin College, Robert earned his master's degree in architecture from the University of Illinois at Chicago and worked for Mies Van der Rohe's firm. During this time he immersed himself in the history of Chicago architecture, from Louis Sullivan to Frank Lloyd Wright,

visiting the neighborhoods of Oak Park and cherishing the clean lines and rich details of Chicago's immaculate urban fabric. As a result of these influential experiences, his design aesthetic embodies a sophisticated amalgam of that rambling, Jersey shore Shingle style and the horizontal banding and craftsmanship found in Prairie style and other contemporary compositions. But no matter the stylistic predilections of his clients, each design takes on a unique storybook quality in which the resulting home truly reflects the intimate stories and lifestyles of the client's life.

Started in 1996, Winters Design Group is a boutique operation in which Robert and Karen Winters design homes for clients based upon their dreams and lifestyles, which provide the design inspiration. The firm's extraordinary designs can be found in Grand Rapids and along Michigan's northern coast, particularly the Harbor Springs area, but past residences have been built in other parts of the country and in exotic locales like Costa Rica. From a recent month-long excursion in Italy Robert and Karen brought back a fancy for durable, enduring architecture and a renewed passion for the celebration of life, a quality they imbue into enchanting spaces that make up their clients' homes.

While Robert deftly conveys the client's personality in the exterior character, Karen designs engaging interiors in which whimsy and surprise await around every corner. Collectively these elements procure homes in which the dreams of generations unfold. Many of the firm's designs are set on bodies of water, and challenging sites provide additional opportunities for extraordinary designs. A recent home built on Lake Charlevoix was set totally on wetlands with two feet of water underneath the house.

The firm is earnestly committed to Green design and building practices, and Robert is en route to obtaining LEED certification. Karen incorporates "recycling by design" into her interior creations, reusing doors, stained glass and other elements in an exceptional manner. Wholly dedicated to fulfilling clients' dreams, Winters Design Group captures life stories in each exquisite home it designs.

ABOVE LEFT:
Nestled on a quaint lake in Michigan, this fire-engine red cottage teases through the trees.
Photograph by Karen Winters

ABOVE RIGHT:
This broad back porch is where the owners spend most of the summer overlooking the lake, enjoying the serene beauty with family and friends.
Photograph by Karen Winters

FACING PAGE TOP:
The interior design of this Bay Harbor residence exudes elegance from the coffered ceilings to the arched bookcases in the library salon.
Photograph by Robert Winters

FACING PAGE BOTTOM:
Set between two ponds, this home met the owners' desire to bring in the dramatic sunsets and sweeping vistas.
Photograph by Karen Winters

DON PAUL YOUNG
TODD MITCHELL YOUNG

Young & Young Architects, Inc.

More than half a century ago, Don Paul Young was loaned Frank Lloyd Wright's autobiography. Captivated, Don realized architecture was the ideal medium to meld his affinity for art and engineering. Compelled by Wright's deft ability to seamlessly amalgamate structure with site, Don has long dedicated his firm to designing sophisticated residences that intimately yet sensitively connect indoor and outdoor spaces.

Don designed and built a 1,600-square-foot house in 1956—an advanced, modern home named one of the 12 best small homes in America by *Better Homes and Gardens*—in which his children grew up and gleaned his appreciation for that vital indoor-outdoor relationship. Moreover, that home served as a catalyst for Don's professional career, attracting clientele interested in not merely building but crafting an intimately tailored house with engaging architectural solutions.

ABOVE:
Fireplaces and a massive chimney separate the four-season room from the family lounge that adjoins the kitchen. Stone floors and wide steps flow through glass walls, allowing a seamless connection from the interior spaces to the exterior stone terrace. The large cantilevered, curved glass overhangs provide sun control, additional shelter and complement the slate roof.
Photograph by Michael Collyer

FACING PAGE:
A beautiful, functional composition nestled upon a knoll, this home celebrates arrival. Spacious and elevated exterior entertaining terraces flank each side of the raised-glass, enclosed living level—all of which is sheltered by strong horizontal lines and the curving slate roof with delicate glass overhangs.
Photograph by Michael Collyer

Don's son Todd, seemingly preordained, took the craft to heart, switching from an art major to architecture, and with his enthusiasm and natural ability eventually earned his master's degree with high distinction from the University of Michigan before joining his father in 1985 when the firm renamed as Young & Young Architects. The resulting synergy from Todd, Don and the Young & Young staff was palpable, as the firm doubled its workload, consistently crafting exceptional buildings in the elusive expression of architecture. In 1992, Don's son Roger joined Young & Young, bringing an invaluable business savvy to manage the firm's ever-growing number of commissions.

Young & Young always collaborates with the landscape architect and interior designer before initial design concepts are formed, devising a three-pronged approach that guarantees continuity from property line to property line. No matter the style, the firm is committed to designing "21st century homes." Even when designing a strongly traditional home,

TOP LEFT:
A peaceful composition of interior spaces enclosed by glass and natural stone, these spaces are protected by a concrete tile roof with large overhangs. The central vertical element is the main staircase connecting all three floor levels. The stairwell is enclosed by a butt-glazed glass corner and translucent red glass "exclamation point" in the center.
Photograph by Michael Collyer

BOTTOM LEFT:
The living room is a comfortable, composed arrangement wherein the architecture, interiors and landscape contribute effortlessly as one to the "spirit of the place."
Photograph by Beth Singer

FACING PAGE LEFT:
A curved sectional sofa within the concave alcove overlooks the indoor swimming pool. Above the sofa is a curved 2,100-gallon saltwater reef aquarium. Structural backlit marble columns dramatically express their purpose as the supporting elements of the structural design.
Photograph by Gene Meadows

FACING PAGE RIGHT:
A ceiling structure of formed cast-in-place concrete supports a circular terrace above with a glass floor, which serves as a skylight permitting natural light to the mosaic glass pool and entertaining complex below. Concentric circles of cushion-edged, French limestone floors, limestone and cast-art glass walls celebrate the use of natural materials. Mahogany French doors lead to landscaped gardens, a fitness center and sky-lit passageway to the residence beyond.
Photograph by Gene Meadows

Young & Young "destroys the boxes." Typically, traditional homes are defined by a large box with more, smaller boxes within—an antiquated, centuries-old approach still widely used today. Conversely, the firm would employ a traditional vernacular yet design open, flowing spaces that are connected thoughtfully to the outdoors via expansive glass so that homeowners are blissfully aware of the natural wonder outside while still retaining the strong, solid masonry forms with their steeply pitched roofs.

From Don's award-winning small home more than a half-century ago to the sublime architecture of Young & Young today, the firm has designed an array of extraordinary buildings for more than 50 years. The additions of Todd and Roger and an experienced dedicated staff to the firm have proved invaluable, taking the practice to a new level while ensuring that the longstanding level of superior architecture continues well into the 21st century.

ABOVE:
This residence located within a gentle hillside celebrates the spirit of organic architecture. There is no interference with the never-ending, continuously flowing levels, overlapping interior and exterior spaces and their quiet connection with the natural surroundings. The result is a highly spatial, three-dimensional residence appearing to hover on its site.
Photograph by Michael Collyer

FACING PAGE LEFT:
This unique boathouse features a large, glass overhead door, permitting direct access to a boat well housing a 40-foot yacht. Panoramic views to the lakefront from the interior and exterior rooms and balconies are evident, yet an intimate connection with the waterfront exists.
Photograph by Gene Meadows

FACING PAGE RIGHT:
This simple, effortless architectural statement is cantilevered above the sand dunes of Lake Michigan, positioned to be a witness and part of "the eternal grand show of planet Earth."
Photograph by Balthazar Korab

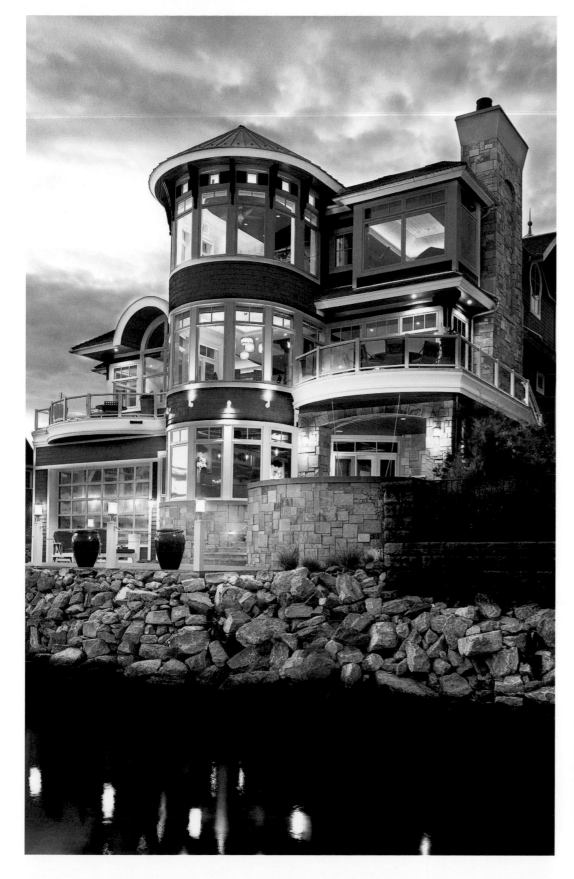

ROBERT L. ZIEGELMAN

Luckenbach | Ziegelman Architects PLLC

Throughout his illustrious career, Robert L. Ziegelman, FAIA, has played an integral role in developing the urban fabric comprising much of Michigan's built environment. Originally harboring ambitions of being an artist as a youth, it was sound motherly advice that steered him toward architecture, which melded his affinity for art with engineering. In the decades since that pertinent realization, Bob's copious designs—themselves works of art—have utilized our three-dimensional environment as their transcendent canvas.

After graduating from Detroit's Cass Technical High School, Bob obtained his Bachelor of Architecture from the University of Michigan and his Master of Architecture from the Massachusetts Institute of Technology. He apprenticed under Minoru Yamasaki and Eero Saarinen, gleaning, primarily, their astute dedication and seriousness to architecture. From Saarinen, he took away his extraordinary ability to develop bold concepts and vocabularies while treating each building as singular and unique. Bob worked on his own for

ABOVE:
The living pavilion's centrally located stainless steel and wood staircase provides a stark contrast between the wood's warmth and the steel's machine aesthetic.
Photograph by Timothy Hursley

FACING PAGE:
An expansive glass exterior enables this vibrant home to shine brilliantly at dusk against its serene backdrop.
Photograph by Timothy Hursley

approximately two decades, then reunited in 1980 with Carl Luckenbach—a fellow Wolverine at the undergrad level with whom he shared a mutual respect—to form Luckenbach | Ziegelman Architects.

In the 1960s, Bob invented a universal building system, which utilized pre-fabricated modular construction and enabled the widespread use of permanent, transportable buildings, significantly reducing waste and allowing for structural flexibility. "I was working with Green before I knew it was Green," Bob says. Originally built for branch banking in Detroit, the system has been used extensively, from classrooms for public schools in Detroit to a pre-fabricated hospital built in Houston and barged to Guatemala.

Early in his career, Bob served with other local architects on the city of Birmingham's Civic Design Committee, developing an urban plan that would be a catalyst for growth and development. He considers it a distinct privilege that he was able to implement more than 37 projects within that urban area, fomenting invaluable urban development in a city where he has lived and practiced. His firm designed numerous Michigan landmarks over the years, including the Kellogg Foundation, University of Michigan business school and the American Axle world headquarters in Detroit, along with residences in Boca Raton, Florida, the beaches of Lake Michigan, Aspen, and the Turks and Caicos.

While commercial buildings account for much of his work, he has created significant residential designs and it is his favorite area in which to work. Though each home is the consummation of a specific site, materials and owner requirements, Bob's designs always engender environments that respond to human values. He tells his clients to "tell us what they want and what their dreams are, and if they write the words, we'll write the music."

One of Bob's more memorable residential designs was an elevated getaway perched in the Rocky Mountains of Vail, Colorado, for a Michigan client. Local design ordinances were geared toward a Swiss chalet aesthetic, but Bob worked within those parameters and still developed an innovative modern form emulating its dynamic natural surroundings. The home was comprised of a group of pavilions resembling mountains—a sublime contextual allusion to its breathtaking natural environment. Built as a vacation home, the client moved into the home permanently upon completion.

Albeit he has already accomplished a lifetime's work in his illustrious career and he and his firm have received more than 90 design awards and national recognition, he is constantly driven to keep inventing unique and responsive architecture—using our physical environment and human aspirations as the backdrop for his enduring art.

RIGHT:
This hallway art niche exhibits museum-grade Native American beadwork at the master bedroom entry.
Photograph by Timothy Hursley

FACING PAGE TOP:
Dynamic, angled ceiling forms are sure to captivate all who enter this engaging kitchen. Interior by Ingles & Associates.
Photograph by Timothy Hursley

FACING PAGE BOTTOM:
The central stainless steel and granite fireplace is a focal point in this living room, which establishes an intimate connection with the tranquil setting outside. Furniture by Ingles & Associates.
Photograph by Robert L. Ziegelman, FAIA

Ken Neumann, FAIA

In Memoriam 1939-2007

During the course of his extraordinary 44-year career as an architect, Ken Neumann, FAIA, did not simply work as an architect—he lived and breathed architecture; it was his passion, his dream and the very essence of his being. Ken dedicated his life to design excellence, and the fruits of his labor stand as a testament to how gifted, amazingly creative and insightful he was. The state of Michigan is privileged to have largely served as the three-dimensional canvas against which Ken's enduring architectural brilliance was deftly wielded, and his impeccable designs will inspire for generations to come.

As an architect, Ken's achievements were illustrious and of the highest merit: he became principal in his own firm before the age of 30; he built a successful business and over the last 40 years served as president, principal in charge of design and a luminary; he was the youngest AIA member ever elevated to its College of Fellows; and he received more than 150 design awards. When it came to design, he was steadfast in his penchant for excellence. If it had his name on it, it had to be right or it had to be torn out. Random color meant

random color, and if it wasn't really random it was gone and done again and again until it was right. But despite that insistence on superior design, he could envision and expound strong design concepts seemingly with ease. When a client was not receptive to the initial design, Ken would simply say, "Let me show you an equally beautiful design," and proceed to redraw the plan—upside down so others could watch—and introduce a bold new idea. Ken was a remarkably talented artist and could draw from every angle, upside down, left-handed—even underwater.

His use of masonry was truly avant-garde, and numerous masonry structures articulated his ideas with grace. Ken said, "Masonry is made of little pieces, but when you put the pieces together, they make magic. You can line them up, turn them on end, angle them, curve them—the arrangements are endless." But no matter the material palette, each structure was borne of a dynamic design concept and metaphorically told a unique story.

For a man with great talent and accomplishments, Ken was truly humble. Harvard-educated, he received such laudable awards as the AIA Detroit Gold Medal, the AIA Michigan Gold Medal, the Martin Luther King Social Justice Award from Ferris State University and the AIA Detroit

LEFT:
A very large house was skillfully organized into smaller-scale elements that are simply but elegantly detailed.
Photograph by Hedrich Blessing Photographers

FACING PAGE TOP:
The hard geometrics of the modernist design are enriched when softened by a curving wave of glass.
Photograph by Timothy Hursley

FACING PAGE BOTTOM:
Overlapping and interlocking space within and outside the building envelope deftly integrate the structure into its site.
Photograph by Timothy Hursley

Blessing Award, but one wouldn't know it by his outward appearance—he was uncommonly modest, kind and fun. Mike Hughes, an assistant vice president at Ferris State University, noted that Neumann/Smith transformed a collection of individual buildings into a campus of remarkable, complementary structures." Ken helped us think strategically to meet academic goals," Mike said. "On a limited budget, he touched and improved every aspect of those buildings and did a first-class job." Ken was also dedicated to passing on his wisdom and ebullience for architecture to younger generations. Mike noted that "Ken never came to campus alone. He was always with a protégé, teaching someone at his side."

Neumann/Smith Architecture continues to build on Ken's legacy of design excellence under the leadership of the talented group of designers who worked closely with him over many years and share his passion for architecture.

INDEX

PUBLISHING TEAM

MICHIGAN TEAM

ASSOCIATE PUBLISHER: Audrey Johnson

REGIONAL PUBLISHER: Kathryn Newell

GRAPHIC DESIGNER: Ashley Rodges

EDITOR: Ryan Parr

PRODUCTION COORDINATOR: Laura K. Greenwood

CONTRIBUTING PHOTOGRAPHER: Beth Singer

PANACHE HEADQUARTERS TEAM

PUBLISHER: Brian G. Carabet

PUBLISHER: John A. Shand

EXECUTIVE PUBLISHER: Phil Reavis

DIRECTOR OF DEVELOPMENT & DESIGN: Beth Benton

DIRECTOR OF BOOK MARKETING & DISTRIBUTION: Julia Hoover

PUBLICATION MANAGER: Lauren B. Castelli

SENIOR GRAPHIC DESIGNER: Emily Kattan

GRAPHIC DESIGNER: Jonathan Fehr

GRAPHIC DESIGNER: Ryan Scofield

EDITORIAL DEVELOPMENT SPECIALIST: Elizabeth Gionta

MANAGING EDITOR: Rosalie Z. Wilson

EDITOR: Anita M. Kasmar

EDITOR: Daniel Reid

EDITOR: Katrina Autem

EDITOR: Amanda Bray

MANAGING PRODUCTION COORDINATOR: Kristy Randall

PRODUCTION COORDINATOR: Jennifer Lenhart

TRAFFIC COORDINATOR: Amanda Johnson

ADMINISTRATIVE MANAGER: Carol Kendall

ADMINISTRATIVE ASSISTANT: Beverly Smith

CLIENT SUPPORT COORDINATOR: Amanda Mathers

CLIENT SUPPORT COORDINATOR: Meghan Anderson

PANACHE PARTNERS, LLC
CORPORATE HEADQUARTERS
1424 Gables Court
Plano, TX 75075
469.246.6060
www.panache.com

Photograph by George Dzahristos

Above: DesRosiers Architects, page 75

PUBLISHER'S NOTE

With its rustic log cabins, beachfront cottages, sophisticated urban retreats, diverse seasons and gentle terrain, the Great Lakes State is the ultimate canvas for dream living. I hope this amazing pictorial journey through these remarkable homes and the extraordinary visionaries who brought them to light will inspire you to create your very own dream home.

Thank you to all of the architects, designers and builders who collaborated with me in creating *Dream Homes Michigan*. Thank you for sharing your unique gifts—for translating dreams and aspirations into reality. Your passion and sincere love of what you do help define where we live, eat, work and play. Thank you to the photographers who have brought these magnificent works of art to life and to my entire production team for all your hard work, support and dedication throughout this fascinating journey.

All the best,

Audrey Johnson

THE PANACHE COLLECTION

Dream Homes Series

Dream Homes of Texas
Dream Homes South Florida
Dream Homes Colorado
Dream Homes Metro New York
Dream Homes Greater Philadelphia
Dream Homes New Jersey
Dream Homes Florida
Dream Homes Southwest
Dream Homes Northern California
Dream Homes Carolinas
Dream Homes Georgia
Dream Homes Chicago
Dream Homes Southern California
Dream Homes Washington, D.C.
Dream Homes Deserts
Dream Homes Pacific Northwest
Dream Homes Minnesota
Dream Homes Ohio & Pennsylvania
Dream Homes Coastal California
Dream Homes New England
Dream Homes Los Angeles
Dream Homes Michigan
Dream Homes Tennessee
Dream Homes London

Additional Titles

Spectacular Hotels
Spectacular Golf of Texas
Spectacular Golf of Colorado
Spectacular Restaurants of Texas
Extraordinary Homes California
Spectacular Wineries of Napa Valley
Spectacular Wineries of New York
Distinguished Inns of North America
Visions of Design
Art of Celebration: New York Style

City by Design Series

City by Design Dallas
City by Design Atlanta
City by Design San Francisco
City by Design Chicago
City by Design Charlotte
City by Design Phoenix
City by Design Denver
City by Design Austin
City by Design Orlando

Perspectives on Design Series

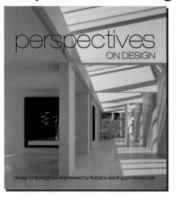

Perspectives on Design Florida
Perspectives on Design Dallas
Perspectives on Design Atlanta
Perspectives on Design New England
Perspectives on Design Pacific Northwest
Perspectives on Design Colorado

Spectacular Homes Series

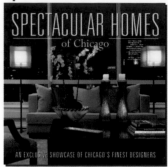

Spectacular Homes of Texas
Spectacular Homes of Georgia
Spectacular Homes of South Florida
Spectacular Homes of Tennessee
Spectacular Homes of the Pacific Northwest
Spectacular Homes of Greater Philadelphia
Spectacular Homes of the Southwest
Spectacular Homes of Colorado
Spectacular Homes of the Carolinas
Spectacular Homes of Florida
Spectacular Homes of California
Spectacular Homes of Michigan
Spectacular Homes of the Heartland
Spectacular Homes of Chicago
Spectacular Homes of Washington, D.C.
Spectacular Homes of Ohio & Pennsylvania
Spectacular Homes of Minnesota
Spectacular Homes of New England
Spectacular Homes of New York
Spectacular Homes of Western Canada
Spectacular Homes of Toronto
Spectacular Homes of London

Visit www.panache.com
or call 469.246.6060

PANACHE
PANACHE PARTNERS, LLC

Creating Spectacular Publications
for Discerning Readers

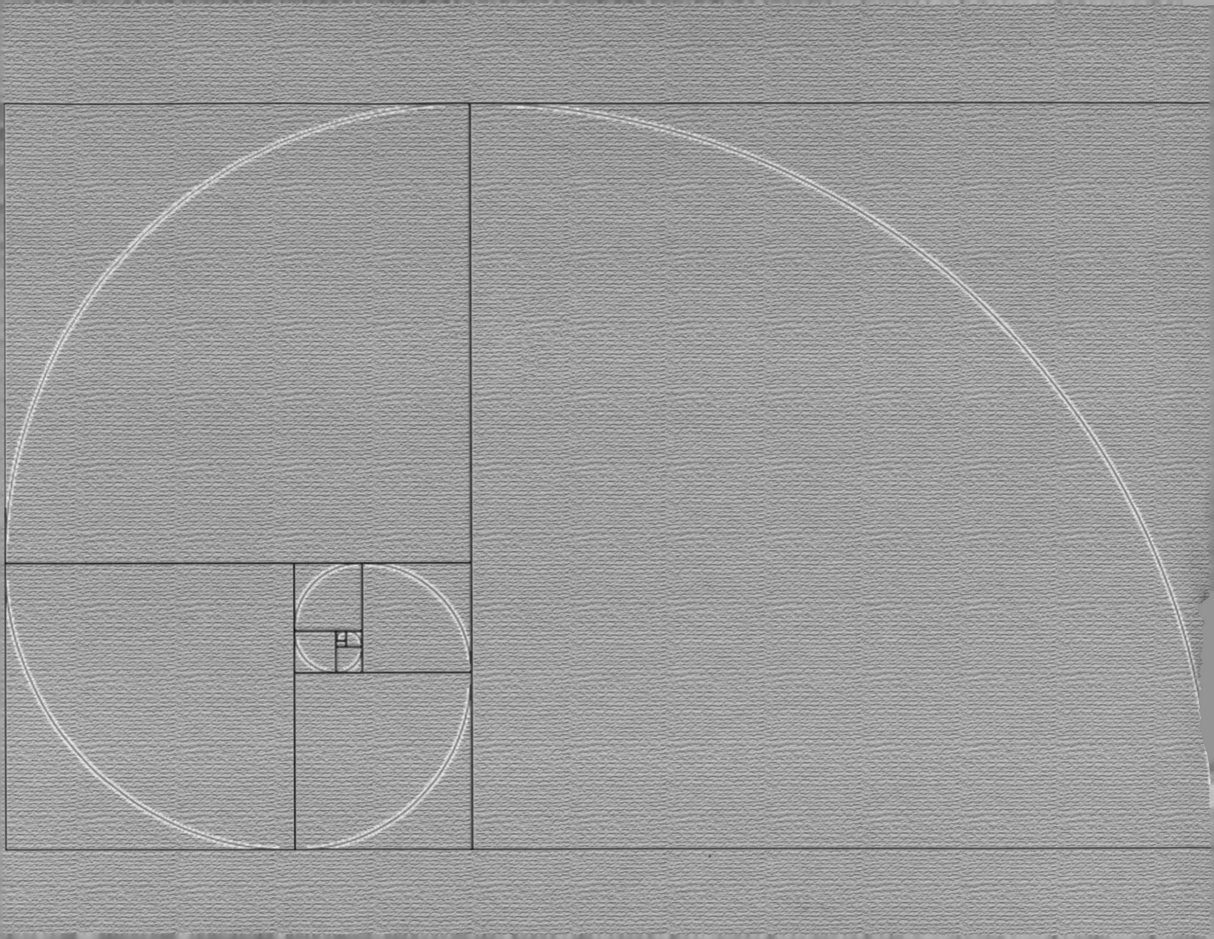